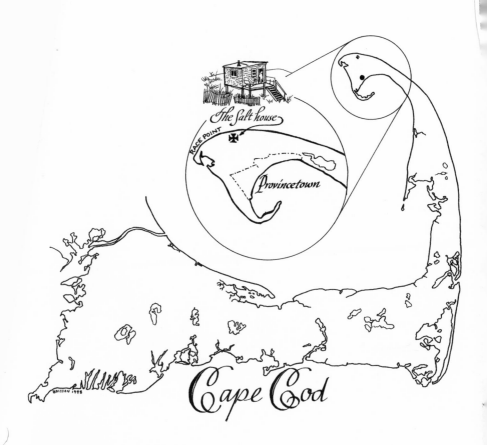

The Salt house

RACE POINT

Provincetown

BRISSON 1998

Cape Cod

The Salt House

The Salt House

A Summer on the Dunes of Cape Cod

Cynthia Huntington

UNIVERSITY PRESS OF NEW ENGLAND
HANOVER AND LONDON

University Press of New England, Hanover, NH 03755

©1999 by Cynthia Huntington

All rights reserved

Printed in the United States of America

5 4 3

CIP data appear at the end of the book

ACKNOWLEDGMENTS

Parts of this work originally appeared in slightly different form: in "The Spiral," in *A Place Apart: A Cape Cod Reader,* edited by Robert Finch for W. W. Norton, July 1993; and "Euphoria," in *Provincetown Arts,* Summer 1998.

For Hazel Hawthorne Werner

The wilderness and the solitary place shall be glad for them; and the desert shall rejoice, and blossom like the rose.—ISAIAH 35:1

Contents

Preface

For three summers I lived with my husband, Bert Yarborough, on the back shore of Cape Cod in a dune shack two hundred yards above the beach, on land owned by the National Park Service. "Dune shack" is the local, and by no means disparaging, term for a certain generation of beach cottages set along the two-mile dune ridge that runs between Race Point in Provincetown and High Head in North Truro, in what used to be the Provincelands State Reservation. Up into the 1920s, the Coast Guard maintained a Life Saving Station near here at Peaked Hill Bars. Many of the shacks were built by the guardsmen as places to bring their wives or girlfriends during their tour of duty, and were later passed down from friend to friend, and sometimes even sold, without regard to who actually owned the land beneath them. They lie along the ridge of the Peaked Hills, at the edge of the dune country that stretches between Route Six and the Atlantic Ocean, at the very tip of the Cape.

Though technically unsanctioned, building on public lands was never considered much of a problem on this part of the Cape. In fact, until near the end of the last century more than half the houses in Provincetown sat on land deeded to the original Plymouth Colony in 1650; in 1893 the state conceded the land beneath the village to its residents. When the Park Service took over jurisdiction of the newly formed Cape Cod National Seashore in 1961, it recognized this tradition of squatter's rights by granting lifetime tenancy to the owners of the shacks. Often built with scrap wood and timbers salvaged from shipwrecks, uneven and raw, wobbly, frequently of eccentric design, they seem unlikely candidates to have endured the ravages of wind and time, yet perhaps a dozen or so still remain in use, continually patched and mended, shingled, shored up, and shoveled out. They remain so for as long as their owners, now grown old, continue to draw breath; they then pass into the hands of the Park Service. Tucked into the hills along the coastline, their roof peaks rising at careful distances from one another, each is a separate kingdom, holding on to its single history, as on to the shifting sand.

The Cape reaches out into the Atlantic from the Massachusetts coast due east for thirty miles, takes a ninety degree turn at Chatham, then proceeds north, flexing in toward the coast as it advances. At Truro the land begins to pull around to form a hook, turning to face the mainland at Race Point and continuing on south and east to Provincetown. Though most of the peninsula sits on a bed of rock left by the last glacier, this final hook is nothing but sand, built up over the past six thousand years from deposits washed along shore by storms and tides. This is where we lived, on no solid ground, at the extreme tip end of the continent, on a bare coast facing north to Greenland. It is a place set apart and bounded by water, where you look west to the coast of North America and the sun rises and sets from the sea. This outpost draws to it various migrants and drifters, sea birds, storm wrack, and tides' leavings, and it was where our life together began.

A great beach, facing the Atlantic for forty miles from Provincetown to Monomoy, finds its endpoint here. The Peaked Hill Bars lie just offshore, extending their deadly shoals for miles out into the ocean. "Mallabarre," Champlain called this coast when he explored it in 1608. Hundreds of ships have wrecked on these bars; their timbers lie buried in the sand. Behind this beach rise eight square miles of dunes and sand plains. All this land is wild, set free by wind and dotted with low growth, lying open under the sun. You step off the highway into the woods and walk a short way between scrub oak, huckleberry, and pitch pines, then you begin to climb a wall of sand. Huge drifts the color of raw silk rise, one beyond another, and the sky is an endless blue. On a hot day, the wavery light rising off the dunes suggests even vaster spaces, deserts of dream floating upward, a moonscape littered with scraps of bone and shell, loomed by cloud shadows, and at the end of it all lies the shining Atlantic, rolling up in scalloped waves against the beach.

Reading over these chapters, taken from our third summer in the dunes, they seem to me a record of some of the richest days of my life. The outer beach sees constant change, exposed to all weathers, tides, and seasons. These pages offer a sort of calendar of our life there, a life that was simple and spare, though never far removed from what we call civilization, in a place of such wild, austere beauty that at first I had no words for its spaces, its dusty heat, the thrilling clarity of its air. Only gradually was I able to take it into myself and let it remake me. My memories of those days are salt, clean and sharp. Days of light and water, salt air, the salt white dunes, the bite of seawater on my skin. Years later, I carry them all in my body, distilled in memory and circulated in the blood.

Bert and I first moved to the dunes ten days after we were married by a justice of the peace in the front room of a rented house in Provincetown, a union even our closest friends predicted would last six months at best. It is possible that bets were taken, though I lack any hard evidence for that suspicion. Never mind, what we had was between us, and we meant not so much to prove anyone wrong as to glide past all predictions into a new adventure. Ours was a quick romance between two people with no discernible plans for the future. Bert is an artist and I am a writer, and we meant to make that the basis of our life together, to invent a life out of what we knew and hoped to discover, making it up as we went along. It was in the dunes where our marriage began, where we learned to love long as well as hard, to live together side by side and work and play. This one-room shack was our only home in those first years—every fall we searched out an off-season-rental, and when spring came we packed ourselves back to the dunes. And so in that sense we thought of it as ours, without ever feeling that we could own it.

It seems to me that the greatest adventure is to find a home in the world, particularly in the natural world, to earn a sense of belonging deeply to a place and to feel the deep response well up within you and become a part of you. When it is done, it can't be lost; the knowledge is as acute and sure as falling in love. What follows is a description of home. We took up residence, not by imposing ourselves on this place, but by giving ourselves over to it and learning what was truly ours.

What was ours was all around us, touching every sense. Glittering beach grasses, and the crying of the terns from dawn to midday, the light and empty spaces of the dunes and the pale line of beach stretching off to the horizon, the constant pounding of the waves, fierce ocean storms that came in and broke over us, and the image of the night sky, endless and bright, coming down to touch the ground all around—all these are deeply ingrained in my being. Days of solitude, walking the shore or writing at my desk under the back window, evenings together in the gentle shadows of the oil lamps—these I will always have. Intimacy with one other, and sometimes terrible silences born of fear or impatience as we learned to live together in a fragile balance of solitude and familiarity. In those rich seasons, if I was unhappy, and, incredibly, I was at times, the fault was in myself, in not being equal to all that was around me.

All of this, everything I have described here, is still as we left it. Who will live there now? Who will see it again? For us, the way our lives are measured, time seems to go forward, but in the wider world it circles and returns. You could go there today and find the same sky, the same waves, the identical birds. It could be yours as it is mine.

More than ten years have passed since we first went to live on the back shore of Cape Cod. As I write this, it is a winter night in New Hampshire, and I am sitting at my desk under bright electric lamps, thinking of the dunes. This night is so cold the thermometer dives below the mind's rational limit of zero, as if it were only possible to gauge negative possibilities of warmth. The snow is piled on the roofs of the houses, and the road snakes black and gleaming between nine-foot drifts pushed up by the plows. The doors of our house are shut and locked, the storm windows fastened, the damper closed in the chimney. Yet even now the surf continues to pound up against the shore, and winter birds circle painfully over the breaking waves. The dunes are locked in their majestic silence, a reticence not of winter, but of eons. The great horned owl rises up from his nest in the oak tree and wheels above the frozen beach, and the shack stands shuttered and small, buffeted by wind, enclosing its dark inner space.

May

What shall I say about Salt House—isolated as a ship, and silent, with the living silence of an audience, though at the same time filled with the unceasing fluid articulation of the sea.

I want to say something important about it, that it has an insistence to drama, exactly in the way that each object stands out in the manner of an arranged and painted still-life . . . The commonplace is defeated here, by I know not what strangeness. Once across the dunes we live in an exquisite unreality.

HAZEL HAWTHORNE,
Salt House, 1934

ONE

The Spiral

We live on the inside curve of a spiral, where the peninsula turns around on itself and curls backward. The tip of this peninsula is still building, extending in a thin line as waves wash sand along the outer shore, nudging it north and west. Moving inward, counterclockwise, the spiral winds backward, to set this place apart in its own self-willed dreaming.

Out here beyond the last bedrock, past the crust of the glacial deposit, we live on a foothold of sand that is constantly moving. Everything eroded and nudged along shore ends up here, broken. Whole coastlines, boulders, good earth perhaps: they all arrive at last as sand. Sand keeps its forms barely longer than water; only the most recent wave or the last footprint stays on its surface.

Sleeping, we wake to sounds of water. Day and night the ocean mutters like a restless dreamer. We live beside it and sleep falling into its voices. Repeating, obsessive, the waves' syllables might almost become words, but do not, just as the sand pushed back and forth at the tide line will not quite hold a form, though the ocean molds it again and again.

At night the oil lamps shine on the boards, and windows hold the flames in their black pools, yellow and welcoming if you were returning here after some journey. The only other lights glimmer down past the beach where boats sail into the night sky; the furthest ones blink like low stars on the horizon. Then one star may take flight, glowing yellow or red or green, and turn out to be a small plane patrolling this outpost, scanning the black water with its radar. The shack rocks gently in wind. Set up on wood pilings against the second dune, it lets the wind under it, gently lifting. We lie apart in narrow bunks like shipmates, breathing softly. Bert turns in his sleep, smacking the mattress with an outflung arm, and the whole bed shakes and resettles. In the high bunk, I feel the shack sway like a boat at anchor, and I know there is nothing fixed or steady, only these currents carrying us along in the dark. The windows are effacing themselves now, as the inner and outer darkness meet at the surface of the glass. I can still see a little bit of sky there; I lift my hand to touch the rough boards of the ceiling, pierced by the sharp points of shingle nails. The boards quiver slightly as night winds blow across them. Wobbling on its axis, the planet twirls off in space, spun in thrall to a star. Only the pull of that great fire, and our opposite thrust away from it, hold us on course.

We live on the outermost, outward-reaching shore of Cape Cod, at no fixed address. In the past three years we have lived in a series of rooms: summer houses in winter, apartments carved out of old hotels, a studio over a lumber yard, all borrowed nests. Of all the borrowed places, this one is best, a little board shack stuck up on posts in the sand, surrounded by beach roses, beach grass and miles of dunes, anchored in sand that flows straight down into the sea.

The shack has a name, Euphoria, which at first struck me as a little silly and high-flown. It means elation, and has to do with the wind. The name came with it, along with other bits of history. In its present incarnation it is the property of Hazel Hawthorne Werner, who holds a lifetime lease with the Cape Cod National Seashore, where it stands. Hazel bought Euphoria in the 1940s from a woman from Boston who had come out to join her lover, who had another shack a ways down the beach. He camped in that shack and she camped in Euphoria until the war came and he went off to fight. The woman from Boston bought it, years before that, from a Coast Guardsman who had built it to house his wife on summer visits. Story has it, she saw the place and promptly fled to town.

Hazel wrote a novel about her life in the dunes in a shack she called Salt House. I like that name, the way it distills the airy ecstasy of Euphoria to something more elemental, a flavor sharper than wind or spirit, preserving the body of the world in something hard and white. The taste of salt is always on my tongue here, held in the air and on every surface, beading my skin. The air has a flavor, a bite; even the sun has edges, reflected and magnified by sand and water. We see more clearly, taste and feel, here inside the salt house of our bodies.

A single room of unfinished boards, Euphoria measures about twelve by sixteen, with a narrow deck in front, facing east, a wall of windows looking north, and a weathervane on a knobby pole, that twirls like crazy in the constant winds. The shack is unpainted except for a little sky-blue trim on the screen door and along the eaves. The rest is the color of old wood—I should say colors, sometimes grey or silver, sometimes brown, depending how much damp is in the air and how the light falls. There are gaps between the boards, and around the doors and windows where sunlight and rain leak in equally; you can look down at the floor and see light glancing through. So it is a not-quite substantial shelter, the idea of a house, but with none of a real house's constriction.

Inside are three tables, one under each window, bunk beds, a gas stove for cooking, and a wood stove for heat. We are equipped with six oil lamps, an enormous kettle bestriding both burners of the range, a dry sink, and a propane refrigerator which invariably breaks down in the heat of August. The front wall faces north across the Atlantic with two big windows we open by tugging on a rope slung over a pulley. Along the south wall another window gazes at the back end of a dune which is slowly collapsing toward the rear of the shack, held back by roots of bay and poison ivy. Day blows straight through when these windows are open, ruffling newspapers and sending loose papers flying. In the most sheltered corner, by the cookstove at the foot of the bunks, a high, narrow window catches the last light of sunset glinting on up-ended pots and pans drying in the dishrack after supper.

From Monomoy to Race Point, surfmen once walked this beach, night and day in all weathers. Twelve Coast Guard stations were strung across a forty-mile stretch, with halfway houses spaced between, where the patrols would meet and turn back. Each night their lights moved north and south, beams of oil lanterns and electric torches, and often a red flare sent up to signal a wreck. Back then these dunes were considered wasteland, though people from Provincetown would sometimes tramp across to cook picnic suppers over a bonfire of wreckage. Townsfolk called this "the back side," the town facing otherwise toward the harbor, and only the Coast Guard walked the beach at night.

Every spring, when the town starts to fill up with people and our winter's lease runs out, we pack up our books and winter clothes to store in a friend's basement and begin assembling provisions for the summer. Out here, the pump handle is screwed together and coaxed into operation, the outhouse retrieved from bushes where it rested on its side, and set up at a discreet distance from the shack. When all is ready, we load our gear on to our friend Bill Fitts's four-wheel-drive truck and move out to the dunes. I unpack what we've brought: rice and oil, and beans, and canned things, books, flashlights, radio, sweatshirts, and things for the beach. Everything fits, in a corner or on a shelf, stowed neat and tight as on a small boat, which is what Euphoria most nearly resembles. I fill the oil lamps while Bert fixes the propane tank to the stove and we're in business. It's a forty-minute walk to town, uphill and down in soft sand—far enough so the summer crowds won't reach us. From here on, we carry our supplies overland in knapsacks—and carry our garbage out—along the old Coast Guard supply route, Snail Road, now just a ghost trail in the sand.

On a still evening, when the wind picks up from the south, we may hear the traffic from the highway pumping into town. From the back shore, it's only two or three miles at any point across to Provincetown Harbor, where the town hugs the bayside and keeps the dunes at its back, and where Route Six, the mid-Cape highway, ends in a parking lot on a public beach. In summer the town fills with tourists and the narrow streets throb with voices and engines. We aren't so far from any of it—the big blue water tower sits on one horizon with the lights of the town ranged beyond it, and Park Service rangers drive down the beach every morning in their green pickups. All summer Air Force pilots train against attack of this coast; their loops and turnings overhead remind us who owns this shore. Grey, sluglike tankers carrying oil from feudal kingdoms lurk on the horizon, and fishing boats trail oil and purple spumes of gasoline. The radar domes in Truro glow at night above the dune called Ararat, and Highland Light sends its white flare around and around, cutting through the clouds with its peremptory beam.

When we have returned from our winter rooms, at the end of another year's wandering, we settle ourselves for a look around, fill the small blue cups with water, and watch as evening comes on. Then it is time to light the lamps, and, not so much later, to put them out.

TWO

Dreamers

I always wanted to live here, even before I knew such a place existed. I dreamed of a cabin: a miniature, makeshift home, and of being a writer and living alone beside the sea. In the dream I assumed I would somehow get here through purity of character and natural destiny, and would live, I suppose, like the lilies of the field—which, I had neglected to notice, curl up and die every winter. The reality is quite different of course, and didn't come by any straightforward means, and not through any virtue of mine to be sure—rather by a combination of luck, accident, and misadventure—real life in other words. Real life provides a sense of progression that dream forgets, a gradual unfolding which in retrospect is liable to seem nearly logical, though we know better. I came here obliquely, by writing poems which I could not publish, holding a series of dead-end jobs, moving around, falling in love many times badly, and finally giving up and falling in love by accident quite well.

Bert and I met at a cookout, my first night in Provincetown. I remember a fire in an oil drum, its metal grill adorned with charred chicken legs and Portuguese sausages blistering with fat, the smell of charcoal and burned meat. I was standing uneasily at the edge of a group of strangers, wondering how soon I could go back to my room without seeming rude, when he approached, holding out a can of beer by way of introduction and looking to my mind like rescue.

I was rebounding—I might as well say ricocheting—from a series of upheavals in what passed for my life at the time. I was newly divorced, after two confusing years during which my husband was more or less missing; that is, he was traveling in India, but I didn't know exactly where he was for months on end. Occasionally he would write to me, on those thin blue, almost transparent air letters that fold over three times on themselves, making a puzzle of their intentions. The letters described temples and train rides, festivals and studies of Sanskrit and Pali, but made no mention of return. Meanwhile, I'd had a brief try at graduate school (I wasn't yet sane enough to discuss the literature I loved, or dutiful enough to read what I didn't love) and a succession of romantic adventures in Michigan, Vermont, and New York, until I was beginning to feel like a poster child for serial monogamy.

I'd left New York that morning, abandoning my bartending job and rent-controlled apartment, along with my last hopes for a foundering love affair, to spend the winter in a single room writing poetry. I arrived with a manuscript, a nine-year-old manual Smith Corona, and two suitcases: all that was left of my material life since college. The Fine Arts Work Center in Provincetown had offered me a writing fellowship for seven months: this distinction afforded me a room above an old lumber yard, with bare floors and ancient, noisy plumbing, two hundred and fifty dollars a month, and the company of other writers and artists in similar straits. This gift of time and good company, which I accepted warily and with little expectation, turned out to be one that would change my life. Within days I decided I would live here forever. This break caught me by surprise and seemed to my mind an unprecedented revelation; I soon learned that it happens quite regularly to people who come here.

Bert was one of the artists who had come and stayed, a sculptor who destroyed most of his own work. He told me he worked outdoors, building sculptures in the dunes and woods, structures of driftwood and branches mostly, materials he gathered along the back shore. I was impressed by the impractical nature of his work, its obvious indifference to any market economy, and all the virtues that implied. We stood talking in the fire-lit dark as people came and went around us. Tall and thin, in a loose sweatshirt and paint-spattered jeans, his pale hair falling forward over the rims of his glasses, he appeared friendly and candid, if perhaps just a little bit excitable. His voice rose and his gestures spilled away from him in all directions as he talked about the landscape where he worked, its miles of dunes and bogs, beaches and scrub woods, insisting that it could not be described. "When I take you out there, you'll see," he promised. It seemed already taken for granted that he would be my guide.

Further conversation revealed that our lives so far had followed similar trajectories, his touching down in several states before coming here, and including two broken marriages and an undisclosed roster of former lovers. We'd both had more addresses than we had lines in our address books. Good sense should have dictated that we take a long look at each other and start running in opposite directions. But that kind of good sense has never interested me. I only remember how he kept looking straight at me the whole time we talked, his eyes, hazel with glints of green, magnified behind thick lenses, as he gestured excitedly with a chicken leg in one hand, toward the side of an empty coal bin, beyond which, I might imagine, stretched the whole wide world.

We met in October, and in December I moved from my single room into the two and a half rooms Bert had rented over a parking lot just off the beach. In love, I fell into slow time, lulled, dreaming of harbors. All night the fog horns kept repeating their hollow assurance: "I am here." The green light of Long Point blinked past the bedroom window and I curled in the dark, motionless, like a mussel anchored to a rock, letting the currents play over me. Day, night, day—where were we being carried? I wondered, dreamed, reached out in sleep to feel for Bert lying next to me, afraid we might drift too far and wake on separate shores.

Mornings, Bert went off to his job, scraping shutters and repainting decks scoured by summer traffic, while I trudged up the street to my lumber yard studio. I worked for hours in that dark, high-windowed room, not so much as glancing up to read the sky, or to follow a flight of wild ducks past the gables of the next house; I worked slowly, greedily, amazed that so much time could be all my own, until a late lunch broke the spell and I surfaced to test the air, throwing the door open with a bang as the wind caught it out of my hands.

Afternoons, I began to walk the beach and the trails leading out from town, and on fine days to climb the slopes of the dunes, their horizons opening before me, one on another. Shaken, the pitch pines gave off a fine white dust of sand from the deep ridges of their trunks, and the heavy dunes lay still up against the sky. I went with Bert when he gathered sticks on the back shore to use for his sculptures, or picked his way through frozen cranberry bogs, scouting the lay of the land. Other days I went alone, along back roads beside marshes where phragmites waved pale, fringed plumes at the sky, down narrow paths pressed by bay and huckleberry, and further out into the dunes, across to the ocean and back again. The winter beach was bare and the ocean glared a cold, metallic grey. The north wind lashed the beach, flinging sand up into my face when I tried to walk against it. There was majesty there, but bleak and forbidding. The back country drew me, with its open, austere spaces; its silences seemed to nurture a suspended life, a place containing more than it revealed. There were no roads there, no electric wires, and because of that, hardly any people, and if it did belong to the federal government, they were mostly leaving it alone. Feeling I could walk there forever, I set out to try.

That first spring arrived in a raw blast of wind and noise as the March winds blared across our narrow strip of land. Skunks paraded out of cellars to pad leisurely down Commercial Street at twilight, their eyes glowing red and unrepentant in the sudden glare of headlights. The town woke up, grew noisy and brusque; hammers rang ownership and prior claims, while shop owners tore the shutters off their buildings and began selling clothes imported from Mexico, and cold soups containing flowers. I blinked in the raw light, like someone waking from a dream. It seemed we had come to the end of something, but where had we arrived? This opening wasn't for us: not for us were mattresses being aired, rugs shaken and window boxes repainted. The price of our two-room apartment spiked upward, renting by the week for twice what we'd paid in a month, and already fully booked through Labor Day. My fellowship was ending, where would I go? What would happen to us? This lack of a home, of any place to be, seemed to me to signal a deeper poverty, an inability to grasp my life and to attach myself firmly to any place, person, or course of action. Perhaps this new life was just another drifter's dream. I had yet to learn that a dream could anchor me, that I might continue to move around a hidden center, and that I would be guided from that center. An idea was just forming: not an idea, but a vision, unsupported by logic or resources, a hope small and dense as a seed; the idea of a life authentic and particular, answerable to nobody, and a home here with Bert, plain and bare, with windows facing seaward. I wished for a sign, and dreamed instead that Bert was standing on a high ladder leaned against a waterfront hotel, holding up a hammer. A huge wind rose out of the sea, and the ladder swayed violently; he called my name and the wind blew his words away.

Hazel always claims she dreamed the shacks before she ever saw them. She was working in New York as an artists' model in the early 1920s while her husband was away crewing on a sailboat. It was a terribly hot summer, and during the long, sweltering nights alone, she would dream of the ocean, picturing a sand bank with a shack perched at the top, and when her husband came back she made him go with her to look for the place she had been dreaming. Having very little money, they walked down the coast from Portsmouth, sleeping on the beach, until they reached Province-town. At Snail Road, Hazel spotted Agnes O'Neill, whom she knew from New York, coming out of the woods with a suitcase. "Hazel, what are you doing here?" she exclaimed, and Hazel re-counted her dream. It so happened that Agnes and Eugene O'Neill were living in the old Peaked Hills Life Saving Station that summer, and Agnes directed them to walk out to the new Coast Guard station. "Tell Mr. Mayo, who's the skipper there, that Gene and I said you were to have one of those little cottages," Agnes told her. The "cottages" rented for twelve dollars a month. Hazel and her husband moved straight into the shack Thalassa, which she later bought for seventy-five dollars. Euphoria came later, years after the husband had gone away for good, and Hazel was firmly enmeshed in another life. But I do think that beginning made her sympathetic to anyone who was actively looking for what they most desired, and ready to take it when they found it.

From the '20s on into the 1960s, Hazel spent her summers in the dunes, walking out from town and back at all hours. She had many lovers, which scandalized the townspeople, then a new hus-band, and then she wrote about it all in two novels, which scandal-ized everyone further. The bookstore in town even refused to sell her second book, which told of her life in the dunes. In her sixties a slow, crippling illness forced her to stop walking the dunes and she moved into a cottage in the Provincetown woods and began to rent her shacks by the fortnight. Finally, at eighty, she talked of closing them down. Unless, perhaps, someone would like to take them over, stay out there all season . . . Thalassa was spoken for, in fact, but did we want Euphoria? It was a hint, an invitation—no, it was an outright gift. We said yes without taking a breath.

Hazel's offer came seemingly from nowhere and seemed to be the very sign I had prayed for. Perhaps she saw in us a shimmer of the passion she had always had, a love of this place itself, along with that longing for freedom which had become almost a first principle of her being. She let us have Euphoria because we were artists, and poor, and in love; because she already knew and liked Bert. But mostly we were right there in front of her and ready to say yes without hesitation. I think I have never wanted anything so much. And so, in fact, it was desire that brought us here, and the dream proved more powerful than any logic, after all.

So we got married and moved to the dunes, joining the ranks of those who lived here before, who built, begged, or borrowed their shacks, stayed as long as they could, then handed them on. I know their names, and some of their stories; many of them have died. There are Frenchie Chanel, Sunny Tasha, Peg Watson, Boris Margo, Dune Charlie, Phil Malicoat, Mr. and Mrs. Roy Hunzinger, and of course, Hazel. Charlie Schmid moved here from New York in the 1950s and bought a shack for one hundred dollars. Charlie lived for his tree swallows; for thirty years he kept logs of their nesting and migrations, built houses for them all around his shack, banded them, and filled pages with records of their broods. His shack is a cantilevered, tilting fantasy of a structure, built from the sky down and balanced against all odds three stories high, empty now, posted off limits by the Park Service. Phil Malicoat came out here to paint great moody, roiling seascapes; he struggled mightily under the influence of his teacher, Edwin Dickinson, like a man who has once touched genius and never found himself the same again. Frenchie rescued birds, nursed wounded animals, and spoke with the dead. Peg Watson, crippled by arthritis, died one winter crawling up the side of a dune after her Jeep stalled on a hill and refused to start again. Harry Kemp drank and strode over the hills with a cape and a staff and wrote awful poems which he signed with a seagull feather, and a man I know only as Louie sat in a fetid single room piled high with paperback detective novels and empty soup cans, its windows scrubbed opaque by years of blowing sand, and listened to shortwave radio eighteen hours a day. Anything was possible. Surely there was room here for our own story to begin.

THREE

Waves

Our first night back, we stumbled over boxes we were too tired to unpack before dark. The room filled with moonlight reflected up from the sand. The clock ticked too loudly, and I got up to put it outside. What possessed me to bring a clock at all? It ends up in the outhouse, singing to itself, time's cricket in a cage, counting the hours with lunatic devotion.

Days pass; we live by the sun. Morning finds us huddled in our bunks, curled against the chill that is May on the North Atlantic. Rising stiffly to feed newspapers and driftwood to the stove, I hear Bert moving in his bunk. "I'm awake," he says, then turns over and begins to snore. I set the kettle on to boil and step outside to brush my teeth on the deck. The screen door bangs shut; a bird cries in the bayberry, far away in its life. A red t-shirt flexes on the clothesline, beach roses open silky petals to the cold salt air, and below the bright, distant sun flickers on the water, glistening blue and white.

The view from the doorstep is perfect, unobstructed in all directions. To the east, a narrow footpath slips between two rose bushes, and winds downhill to the pump. A meadow of beach grass stretches along the foredune, cut by the soft white line of the path that climbs toward the horizon and disappears. The beach itself I can't see, because it drops off beneath the hill, undercutting it. Behind me, sand dunes lift and heave up bare, one beyond another, softly mounded forms, sixty, sometimes eighty feet high, that loom and bulge up against the sky.

These sand dunes were made by the ocean. They are ground the sea gave back, returned from every shore its storms have ripped or currents tugged or tides unraveled, and it is an odd, sometimes unearthly-seeming place. The dunes rise up like monuments; the ocean took thousands of years to build them, but they may be seen, in slow-time, to breathe and move, rising and falling and lapping forward. Now in spring the skittish birds touch briefly and lift off again, leaving scratches in the sand. Waves push up against the shoreline, and beneath the waves, with every beat, a new line of dunes is forming as a sandbar slowly rises offshore.

When the ocean makes land it creates something different from land's land. No bedrock or heavy humus and clay, no hard-packed soil to clasp the roots of big trees and fold records of time in its layers. It builds with what its currents can carry, piece by piece, and grain by grain, slowly accumulating. The ocean, in its disquiet, can only imagine—that is, bring forth an image of—flux, and so it creates a shoreline that moves in waves, and hills that rise and fall and toss over one another, and take the print of the wind on their surfaces.

From where I'm standing, the landscape presents a peculiar unity. My gaze takes in dunes and ocean, miles of water and sand lapping in either direction. They look like images of one another, though the dunes lie still and the waves keep churning toward shore. This is an illusion, of course; in fact it is the dunes which are moving, some fifteen feet a year, walking south toward the highway, headed for town. The water's not going anywhere; a pulse moves through it, lifts, and lets it go. In a time-lapse photo, over a season, or a year perhaps, the impression would be re-versed: the waves must freeze to an average stillness, a little blurred at the edges, and the slow-moving dunes would be seen to crawl forward, cresting and tumbling over themselves, grain by wind-borne grain. Quietly, in smallest increments over millennia, the wave turns to stone, and the stone dances.

Wet grains of sand are sharp and cold, clinging to the soles of my feet as I make my way down to the outhouse. The clock on the ledge, "Little Ben," shows a quarter past six. At the bottom of the path I pause to look out across the marsh below, all pale green over grey-shadowed sand, and back into the dunes where a hundred seagulls are stirring from their nighttime roost. They rise and begin wheeling down to the beach, making sleepy grumbling noises as they fly across the sky, the sunrise rosy on their breasts.

Every night after sunset they leave the shore to fly back into the shelter of the dunes. Day turns them and they rise, circling down to the water's edge, adding their constant motion to its rhythms. Now they lift and begin to turn, veering off to the east, a dark cluster opening, spun outward like a spiral galaxy. Nothing organizes them; the figure unfolds in an instant out of separate bodies, a starflower blossoming, charged with light. They come and they come, lifting my sight after them; now their cries sound across the hills. They are, briefly, one thing, then just as quickly the form dissolves as they spread across the sky and are gone. I feel a chill along my skin, like fear: I look back, and there is no mark where they slept against the side of the dune, a hundred white birds covering the sand. The sky is full of them, and then empty.

The cold of these mornings gets into my bones, I think, when I feel how lightly the world holds us, how quickly we pass through it and are let go. Our whole presence here is momentary; we cling to the side of a dune in our little wooden shack, and call it home. We invent our own story, in its thousand details, accumulating particulars to construct a life, each day remade in its own image. A wave, a ripple, a shape of wind. Does a shack on stilts in sand leave a mark? Or the way we touch each other in the dark? This is our third summer here: I wonder what shape we make, what gesture holds.

I latch the wooden door behind me and turn to climb the path. Little leaves of ivy threaded with strands of beach grass flip and shiver in the breeze, showing their dark undersides to the light. A

ripple passes along the hill, a scutter of light across surfaces wet with dew, as the birds tilt white bellies, grey backs overhead, a visible wave taking on various bodies as it moves through the world.

The ocean is waves and the dunes are also waves: are they a form or a motion? Cadences of water and rock echo each other in slow time, while the gulls' wings make a figure I can only see clearly in my mind, a shape that exists nowhere, caught in the instant of opening, closing. Yet the world is real, repeating its coherent patterns. A pulse thrums through bare matter, arranging visible molecules in its reflection, adding a curve to every line—it beats through us and we're lifted, carried forward, reeling. For every fall forward is a compensatory holding back, a hesitancy in matter that makes it circle back to complete itself. Straight lines are the mind's fantasy; the world is round and we move in orbits, revolving away from a center we do not see, and "the way from any point to any other point," as D. H. Lawrence wrote, "is around the bend of the inevitable."

Thunk up the stairs; the smell of coffee advancing on the air encourages me that Bert is up and life goes on. "Good morning!" I call, peering in through the screen. A muffled reply issues from the far corner where he stands with a towel over his face. Water splashes in the basin, then the little clink and scrape of razor and mug. "You stay put," he sternly admonishes the mirror leaned against the shelf. I sit down to brush the wet sand from my feet. A thousand particles, clinging to whatever touches them, travelers from a thousand shores, they fall back into an ocean of sand.

If this world moves in waves, sand is the matter that is displaced, lifted grain by grain, in minutest particles, singly and in droves, to change the structure of appearances. Sand follows motion; nearly weightless, it can blow away or float or be carried along in any movement of air or water. Old eroded crystals, granules of rock, particles of quartz and feldspar, flakes of silica, they are nothing alone. Together they create a landscape. Gathered up,

they make plains and pleats, cliffs and dunes, and long sloping beaches where terns and plovers scratch out their nests in summer. Sand grains are very old, worn down from rock into particles, finally nearly irreducible. They are the particular, the acted-upon, *material*. Whatever force moves through us, without these particulars to gather and adhere, our days are lost, blown away in a motion too great to hold. So too the thousand things: the chill of daybreak giving way to sun, casting deep shadows in our footprints tracked across the sand and back, the tightly gathered petals of the beach rose opening, the woodstove sending its plume of smoke from the chimney.

Bert's voice comes suddenly from the doorway behind me. "So, how did you sleep up there?" he asks. Any movement in the bunk by either of us sets the whole contraption shaking, but Bert thinks I'm the only one who moves.

"I slept just fine," I answer him mildly.

"Well, you were flipping like a pancake. I thought the bed was going to come down." His voice is teasing, inviting response. So the domestic current resumes, with its tug and press: affection and challenge, call and response. The two of us swim in it, rise and fall, and feed in its streaming. This current carries us forward; we're held in the wave as it breaks and falls. I brush the numberless grains from my toes and stand up, turn, and walk full circle into my lover's arms.

FOUR

The Edge

The beach goes on forever, a membrane between two worlds. I walk that disappearing line, along the edge of it, where the water slams up on shore and its movement reverberates through my entire body. A billion grains of sand shift underfoot and cold water crashes at my feet, once every seven seconds. This is no-man's-land, where nothing grows, a place of contention and disorder, of broken forms, and litter that stinks in the sun. Here the great beat of the ocean falls back, finding its limit; the waves curl as they hit and burst into particles, tossing molecules of water and salt into the air. The shore thrums softly with each blow, and, sloping downward, dives under water. And in all this beat and surge the victims are casually cast up, things of one world that can't live in the other.

Bodies float up and begin to rot in the rich air. A new moon pulled the tide high up the beach last night, leaving long, scalloped ridges of wrack and flotsam to mark its retreat. Shells with their insides gone soft and black, wet crumbling snail meat, and unhatched fish eggs all bloated and stinking in their sac membranes, lie strewn across the sand. A kind of sponge called dead man's fingers swells and dries pale in the sun, a six-fingered amputee, porous and reeking. The upper beach is studded with debris: nests of driftwood, cans, and dense, salt-rotten boards, bottles ground to a dull sheen by the waves' thrashing, tangled string and garish shreds of fishnet dyed orange and red, acid yellow, and the dire green of deepest sea caverns. I kicked up a light bulb wrapped in black electrical tape and sticking half out of the sand, a glass mummy loosening its bandages. These things belonged once to the land and were lost. They return strangely changed, with the smell of that other world all over them. A snarled fishing line, trailing a plume of kelp and a plastic detergent bottle, slams back and forth in the shallows; up ahead in the sand, something small and ghostly is burrowing out of sight.

It's a bright, cold morning down here among the wrecks. I'm walking at a slant, left foot low, right foot high, one side to the water and one leaning upland, heading east and south towards Truro. The high beach is flatter, but the sand up there is soft; here at the waves' edge is firmer footing. Up ahead in the east, the sun spreads an oily sheen across the water. The sky is pale, with a foam of sea clouds stirred into it, as if someone had poured white paint into blue without mixing them thoroughly. Along the horizon, a thin white line appears, tracing the border of sea and sky, a gap between the worlds where another light shines through.

Past the opening where Snail Road cuts through the foredune, an intersection marked by two posts in the sand and some jeep tracks that end abruptly at the tide line, I press forward into an empty landscape. Three gulls ride high above the waves, their wings barely moving as they float on an offshore breeze. The shoreline stretches away in an arc, following the curve of the earth, and drops down into the sky. Down here only the barest coordinates mark a position—there are no landmarks, everything flat and bright. My hand above my eyes, I scan the front of the sand bar, hoping for a glimpse of whales, but it's still too early. The finbacks will be here in June.

In late May the back shore is almost empty of life. The spring migrations raced through in April: geese and arctic terns headed to the northern tundras and cold inland lakes of Canada and

Greenland. In town their hurried night flights woke us; cries of passage echoed in our dreams. Deeper inland, warblers streamed through the woods, flitting in and out among the spiky branches of pine and beach plum. Blackburnians, magnolias, blackpolls, and Tennessees, they rested, fed, and moved on, followed in turn by our summer residents, the kingbirds, catbirds, phoebes, and swallows, who are gathering now in woods and marshes along the highway. Most of our ocean birds have disappeared—even the herring gulls, who seem otherwise never to forsake our company, have begun scattering to nesting colonies along Monomoy and Long Point. Today a few immature gulls, too young to breed, strut importantly down the beach, meeting up with a company of the smaller, pretty laughing gulls, just in from the Carolinas.

Some birdhouses poking up over the hill were the first sign I was nearing Thalassa: gradually the peak of its roof rose into view above the crest, then came a small dip in the grasses where the footpath winds down the hill, not noticeable really, unless you know how to look for it. The passage of people over sand is ghostly, fleeting. Where Frenchie's shack faces the beach, thrusting its little screened porch out ahead of it, the dunes open slightly to allow a glimpse of its shingled front. Years ago a sand dune moved in and covered this shack, burying it up to its windows, and rather than dig it out whoever owned it then simply built on top of it, making this the only shack in local record with a basement.

Past Frenchie's, still shuttered and dark inside, and past Thalassa, with its little pointy roof rising over the foredune, around the bend and beyond the cliff where the beach gets narrow and almost disappears at high tide, some terns were flying, making high, nervous cries above the whitecaps. These were least terns, little sea swallows with black caps, forked tails, and temperaments as quick and tense as bees. They seem to dislike the land, and only come on shore reluctantly to nest, where they exhibit all the paranoia of exile. They began arriving last week from South America, and are getting ready to mate and scratch out their nests on the sand. One would approach the shore and veer off, as if losing nerve, then turn and take it out on his neighbor, wheeling and crying out in an accusing tone. By midsummer their nervousness will flower into a hysteria that will send them diving at the heads of intruders, but today they only followed me complaining, making a quivering company along shore. And when they had had enough of me, they flowed away into the sky.

After the terns I saw no one, just a disconsolate crow jabbing at a reeking pile of eel-grass, and a half-dead skate I nearly stepped on at the water's edge, a flat, gelatinous carpet heaved up cold on the wet sand. I stopped and poked it with my foot, and it rose up with a shudder, revealing its white underside, its gaping v-mouth gulping the fatal air. From deep covered sockets on top of its head its eyes stared and rolled as the thing with a prodigious effort flipped on the sand, lashed its horny tail and fell back. That must have been the last gasp because the next wave lifted it and it rode back and forth in the waves, its wings flopping uselessly.

My shadow trails me as I walk south. There are no shacks out this far and little sign of life. The beach gets narrow, then wide again; grass grows down to the tide line, then the shore is cut back in a steep scarp sloping upward for a hundred yards. Along the rim where waves have torn at the edge of the grasses, black, salt-soaked roots hang exposed in midair. A plover skids past with a plaintive cry. Where am I? I could be anywhere. The scene is all flatness and falling away—the empty strip of beach running down the side of the globe, and the blue dome of sky curving down to meet it. Past Pilgrim Heights, maybe, certainly not so far as Head of the Meadow. I can't be sure. What at a distance seems to be a wreck unburying itself turns out, as I approach, to be a tree limb bucked about in the waves, A whale's carcass rises out of the sand, but as I come closer it becomes a bleached log, salt white, with stubs of broken limbs.

I stop and open my water bottle. The tide has turned, and small waves wash up over the hard berm. Teasing the edge, they sizzle, fizz, and run back down to the water. Behind me, I notice my footprints running at an angle up the beach, swelling and darkening as water rises in them from below. Without my paying attention, the incoming tide has pressed me higher inland as I walked. This visible evidence of change is unexpectedly startling. "Time and motion, time and motion . . . of course," I think, to reassure myself.

Here is the point of creation, a beat that has been going on since time began. The present: breaking, moving, clashing, never to be repeated; the world teetering on a point of balance. The waves make old music, tearing at the shore, singing, "you must change, change," as they press forward on the land, a movement widening, center to circumference, opening until it breaks. Offshore a small boat drifts east with the current; there's a dragger about a mile down, in close pulling for scallops. Overhead, a pale broad sky floats off into space, not even seeming to touch the horizon.

The sun is high now; I need to think about heading back. If I turn around the scene will all be new, this sheet of sand before me, the endless border of sea and land, and offshore a green curl of wave breaking over the sandbar. You can't bend time backward; even the way home is another going forward, and the waves never repeat, or rest. One curve leads to another, endlessly disappearing. I walk, balanced on an invisible line that only exists in motion. And wherever I step, waves are tearing the ground away beneath my feet.

The sky is cold; its air is thin. I walk in the sky, bathed in sky, holding onto this narrow shore where the sea approaches and retreats before me. A line of sand grains forms at the shoreline and presses inland, a single line, then another. I give a moment to looking both ways, but I walk the edge, my head turned toward the path, the line without width or depth. The beach goes on forever and I walk that disappearing line, into time that opens to the pressure of my passing and closes behind me, complete.

FIVE

Harrier

The marsh hawk is back. We've missed seeing her these first few days and worried that she had gone off. But this morning she flew in from the west, crossing in front of the windows where we sat eating breakfast. For a moment the air was full of her, a large brown beast, warm and strong with life, charging the space between us with a fierce resolve. "The hunter," Bert said as she flew close, her wings spread wide. We could see the determined hook of her beak and the small, pale eyes fixed in concentration as she beat steadily westward.

"The" marsh hawk, I said. There has always been a marsh hawk at Euphoria, according to—well, everybody. The landscape seems to require one, this bare hill giving way to valleys spotted with rose and bayberry, and the beach meadow that stretches for miles down the coast, whose high grasses shelter mice, voles, shrews, and other small creatures, a regular rodent buffet in summer. Hawk, mice, rabbits, moles and shrews—they have been entwined here for generations, maintaining a bloody equilibrium on this narrow strip of earth.

There's no way of knowing for sure whether this bird is the same one we've seen the past two summers, but it probably is. She's a big female, almost two feet long, with a wingspan more than a yard across. She winters in the woods near town, around Clapps or Shankpainter Pond. I think I have even seen her there, hunting along the highway down by Herring Cove. Summers, she nests in the marsh behind Phil Malicoat's shack—that's the direction she comes from as she crosses the dunes every morning. She appears rising up from the bog behind us, passes in front of the windows, and flies up the coast along the outer dune ridge. Her routine never varies: always a quick flyover in the morning, intent on reaching some distant spot, and then a more leisurely afternoon call when she pauses to hunt close to home.

The marsh hawk is not an especially rare bird, and not the biggest one here, either. The great horned owl is more imposing, and people have even spotted eagles in the woods not far from here. But this hawk is important, a part of the place's story. We look for her return to mark our own, to verify our place in the succession of residents at Euphoria. She is part of our life too. For two summers now we've watched her, learned her habits, stood struck still with the beauty of her flight as she threaded in and out among the hills. Her arrival completes a circle we stand just outside of—witnesses or citizens, we're not always sure. Who holds a true title here? We're all transients, still squatters when all's said.

We finished breakfast and hurried outside. First down to the beach to pay our respects to the Atlantic. A path one footprint wide draws a faint white line through the waving green, then opens onto bare sand.

When you get to the ocean there is nothing to do but stop and look at it. It is a cold sea, bright with reflected light; your gaze glances off its surface, skids across the deep closed darkness beneath. You can look and look, without seeing any more. This morning the surf was sending up a dull roar, broken from time to time by the hard thump of a breaker collapsing on the packed sand. Wind out of the northwest stirred the waters into a froth, whipping the hair into the corners of my eyes.

We stood together with our arms crossed over each other's backs, and watched a big, awkward gull being driven slowly backward by the wind.

"Do you want to walk with me?" I asked.

"I don't think so. I need to go back and look at those drawings I did yesterday. See if they're doing anything. You don't mind?"

I don't mind. We've both learned that life in small quarters depends on each of us spending time alone every day, and Bert knows I like to walk in the mornings before I write. We stood leaning on each other a while longer, braced against the wind, then gradually unlocked our arms and moved apart. He kissed me, and we turned to go our separate ways. Bert took the tight winding path up through the beach grasses, and I headed into the wind, going north.

I worked my way down the beach for about half a mile, the wind pushing against me, cold air filling my lungs. I pushed back, leaning into it with each step. Dry seaweed blew down the shore, making little scuttling sounds. The beach was wild, edgy, cold. A little ways up past Phil Malicoat's, I turned into a gap between the dunes. Behind the first wall of sand the world was quiet again; the sun fell warm on my hands. The grasses stood up straight and still in the sun—new green shoots pushing up into a nest of last summer's dry stalks. Rabbit scat dotted the edge of a plum thicket. The beach plums were stark and wintry looking, with little leaves opening along their spiky branches.

It's spring, such as it is. Springtime lags four or five weeks behind the calendar here. The surrounding waters, which keep the air mild, and warm rosebuds into December, can't forget the injury of winter, and remain a grudging reservoir of cold through June. The sun pours down and the water glares back, then turns a cold shoulder of wave upward. In April the average temperature in town is forty-four degrees, in May about fifty-five—but don't count on it. If you need to feel sure of spring on Cape Cod, look to the return of the light, which is ordained and measurable, and ignore, if you can, the fickle winds.

I came up behind Phil's along a sort of path marked by a broken section of old fence running along a ridge. The shack has been opened, but nobody is staying there now. Since Phil died last year it has sat empty most of the time: his family can't get used to the place without him.

Hunkered down behind half a dune, Phil's is a grand shack, with two rooms, one with a brick fireplace and the other boasting a big-bellied stove. It also has a flush toilet in a little bathroom underneath, which I found most impressive when we visited him there. It works by gravity; you empty a pail of water into the toilet and it all goes down a pipe and ends up God knows where. Of all the shack owners, only Phil Malicoat ever owned the land he built on. He bought a pie-shaped plot running from the bay side to the back shore in the 1930s for a hundred dollars. (He said he had to borrow fifty.) Townspeople thought he was crazy, buying land no one wanted, but he ended up with bayfront and oceanfront property, as well as all the woods and dunes in between. And when the Park Service drew up plans for the National Seashore in 1961, they found Phil's land slicing right through the middle. He struck a bargain, selling off most of the dune acreage to the Park Service, and kept the shack to hand on to his family.

Phil liked to walk the beach every morning; however early we came out we would always find his footprints ahead of us in the sand. After breakfast he would drive his old green Land Rover back into town, where he would paint all day in his studio. We miss his wild evening rides, when he'd appear careening over the top of the big dune, gunning down Snail Road and then up the beach, which he drove like a dragstrip, and his two-minute visits to drop off a gift of lettuce from his garden, or in August the inevitable zucchini. He would never stop to talk, or even turn off his engine, impatient to get back to his shack in time for sunset. He was seventy-two, with a bad heart, when a stroke felled him near the end of winter. Now in the mornings, our prints are the first ones on the beach, an honor we never earned, or much desired.

Skirting the marsh, with its cranberry bogs and high-bush blueberries, soggy with rain this time of year, I climbed up into the dunes. The sand is loosening underfoot as the sun dries it, scuffing up a finer dust as it changes from brown to ivory. It is as if no one had ever walked there, when the dry wind lifts away your footprints and the herring gulls scud overhead with their prehistoric beaks and astonishingly white, wide wings. The long dune shoulders rise and fall, bare, trackless, and the whole wide landscape seems to flow out in all directions, with nothing to stop your gaze from rolling down the side of the earth. I walked along kicking at bones the wind uncovered, poking my nose into white bits of shell, and green upstarting in clumps. Light and shadows crossed the sand; the dunes tilted up into the turning sky, folding one into another. I climbed them as if launching myself into space, into air so sharp and thin it hurt to breathe. Nothing was holding me. The sweet pitch of a blackbird's voice rose up from the marsh below.

At the summit, I turned and saw in the distance the pale, still line of the beach molded to the changing water. To the right a jeep trail cut into the sand; two stripes of tire track humped up in the middle, headed straight down the side of the dune and disappeared into a miniature woods of oak and pitch pines. To the left, in the distance, the blue water with its border of white sand, the beach grasses waving together at the sky, and Phil's shack riding the saddle of the dune, its fine brick chimney pointing to the sky. Further to the east, sticking up behind another dune, I could just make out the slanted roof of Euphoria, looking for all the world like a crude spacecraft hastily parked there.

That is where I live, I told myself. What a small bit of world it is, seen from such a height. A clearing around a little cabin. A room plain and bare, where Bert sits drawing, hunched over scraps of paper on the floor, a stick of charcoal clenched in his fist. But everything is there, our lives, our objects, the spaces our voices form around us. Not the place, but the life it holds, how we move through it, what we do there, what we remember. Four walls and an open door, a living presence within. Without that it is just a dot on the landscape, a still point not to be noticed, a box of air.

My gaze flew out over hills and valleys, and down across the beach. I was up so high I might have been flying, or falling, and as I stepped forward along the crest of the dune, striding east with the wind pushing me, I opened my arms for balance and rose, catching an updraft, and sailed east up along the coast. Ahead of me Euphoria lay half-hidden on its crest; I blew past the woods' edge, circled over the water and back, wheeled in, and flew on-ward like a hunting bird, fixed on that central spot. Grey boards, grey shingles, dark glint of windows. I flew on down the other side of the dune and came back to myself again and met my body walking in the furrows of a jeep trail that curved through pines and bayberry, trudging in soft sand, still heading home.

Cocktail hour. I've got a pot of chili simmering on the stove, and a cup of cool pump water by my hand. We sit on the top step gazing out; shadows race across the stony dunes and behind us the shack trembles slightly, holding its shape against all that blows.

Bert is showing me the drawings he worked on this morning. He started them in the dunes yesterday, pieces of landscape abstracted in ink. I recognize gestures of beach grass, and the scratchy, dry branches of a dead bayberry. They're spare and direct, with graceful lines, small pieces of the world lifted out of context.

"I like them," I say, turning over a page.

"I don't know, they might be too pretty," he worries.

"They're simple," I say, "clear."

"Hmm. You know, there's simple as in 'easy'. Take the world as you find it, just render, appreciate everything. I don't like that. I want something more single-minded. Clear down to the bone." He stretches out his legs and looks around.

"It just seems there has to be some urgency, or necessity. I'm not sure if these do that." He squints again at his drawings, then gathers them up to take inside.

"Stir the chili while you're in there!" I call back over my shoulder. "Stir it with urgency."

He comes out. "Do I have time to walk down to the beach before supper?"

"Hours," I say, giving a magnanimous wave and leaning back against the step.

Sitting here, watching him go, I feel a righteous tiredness and a heaviness in my body, especially my legs, after this morning's long walk across the dunes. Walking in sand is incredibly good exercise. With every step your foot gets partly buried, and in order to move forward you have to dig it out and push off with a rolling motion that uses every muscle from the hips down. My friend Wally Tworkov, who comes to Provincetown every summer with her husband Jack, keeps warning me not to get what she calls "dune legs." I'm not sure exactly what she means—presumably an overdevelopment of the calf muscles, or maybe a thickening of the ankles from this constant, odd exertion—and I don't know what I can do about it anyway. She says she's seen it happen: even to Hazel, the beautiful Hazel, though I must admit I've never noticed.

When I visit Wally each spring, she glances up and down my whole body appraisingly. She says it hasn't started yet.

Bert is walking away across the sand. I watch him go. His back-lit shape recedes and darkens as he goes down the path. The sun is still high at five o'clock, but a chill is climbing up from the beach. I see his strong back, his loose stride, as he climbs toward the horizon of dune and sky and disappears over the edge.

She floats up the side of the hill and wheels around, circling the meadow, not making any sound. Her wide wings tilt upward in a shallow V, draped on the air, barely moving. The sun casts a reddish light on the grasses, which seem to shiver, and everything stops breathing. She banks to one side, showing her white rump, the streaked brown of her belly, and the world tips under her and slides, ever so slightly, to the west. She dips out of sight behind the foredune and I wait. Once I would have dashed for the binoculars and followed her flight in and out among the hills, hungrily, as if I could put some sort of claim on seeing her, or as if she could give me something. I was still a tourist here, collecting sightings for the life-list, checking off tidbits of lore and scratching for hidden meanings. Now I just watch her, feeling a kind of friendliness. We see each other. I doubt she can tell me from any other human residents at Euphoria, anymore than I can be sure this is the same hawk who was here last summer. But that doesn't matter: I like how she takes my presence for granted, assumes we both belong here.

She comes back and holds her course along the crest of the dune. The hunter. Here is a clarity with no ease or sentiment. She is a heat, a pulse, all muscle, heart and sinew, fire in her eye. Bert will see her now if he turns around, our gazes crossing in the air to follow this third, turning point. This looking together from two places must send up a charge, a sort of spark to lift our everyday awareness into a vivid moment of presence. Looking from two places, holding her image between us, things might stop a minute; we might be offered a glimpse into another order.

Pass after pass across the meadow, everything goes quiet before her. The grass is alive; small hearts beat in hiding as she stitches back and forth. In the quiet she listens, then pounces, talons outstretched. She beats the grass with her wings, wrestles the air and rises up with nothing. Flapping her wings lightly, she sinks down on to a bayberry to compose herself. She folds her wings, gripping the branch, and rests, still hungry.

Is this the same hawk who has always been here? Yes. She is a door in the sky, opening to a lineage of hawks, and as we watch her we are pulled through that doorway into the other world.

It's getting cool. I sit in the shadow of the shack, facing into the northeast, the sun already gone overhead, with food cooking on the stove inside, and I turn my face to the path where Bert will be returning. The marsh hawk is flying up the coast now, following the arc of some long circle. She is flying west into the blaze of the afternoon sky, a dark shape just skimming the hill. I feel my bones, and the good boards under me, and the cold in the sea-wind rising. It's coming on to suppertime; we're having chili. I leave her to chase down her bloody feast, and go in to see to ours.

June

I Have Found Out

I have found out in love a little flattery
Turns out much better than assault and battery.

—HARRY KEMP,
Poet of the Dunes, 1952

SIX

❦

Nesting

The redwings down by the pump are squabbling again and chasing one another uphill and down—a quarrelsome household. Just now the female broke angrily through the leaves of the bayberry and darted uphill, flying low to the ground, followed closely by her mate who scolded her in short harsh syllables, then dove down to strike her with his beak, as if that settled matters. They set up housekeeping in the big bayberry bush last week, and since then it's all been chase and flick, display and whistle, as the breeding season gets underway. A kingbird interrupts his vigil on top of a pine tree to threaten me with an acrobatic tumble through the air when I pass, and the catbird sounds a wheezy alarm from the plum thicket. Yesterday the goldfinch took up his courting from the top of the weathervane. Though they won't nest until late summer, the male begins his love song early, singing lustily from the highest spot he can find. Warbling from that shaky perch, he's hopping about in his bright new yellow plumage, turning one way and then another, desperately showing off.

We return each spring with the birds, who come back each year to the same place. When swallows move into the garages in town, preening and twittering, and redwings mass noisily in tree tops alongside the highway, we come too and shake out our nest to begin the season.

When I watch nesting birds, their uneasiness always strikes me first. The demands of the season—its passions if you like—seem to go against the grain with them. They return all full of journeys and long distance, the light of horizons glinting in their sharp eyes. They don't seem to like each other very much, but to answer some drive stronger than personal preference. This puts them on edge, both attracted and irritated by each other's presence. The kingbirds who arrive in April to nest in the pine woods are so territorial it's a wonder the species has survived this far. At first the male attacks the female and chases her away. He has to be convinced that she is not a competitor, his suspicions worn down through sheer persistence on her part, until finally he lets her into the territory and they build a nest. Then she turns the tables, throwing him off the property until the eggs hatch. They somehow manage a brief truce during which they cooperate in feeding their young, a forced accord broken by much arguing and complaint, and flights across the hillside to gaze longingly into the distance, dreaming of another life. Even the mild-mannered song sparrow is given to sudden rages now; without any warning he leaves off singing and flies at his mate, screaming, even pouncing on her, as she flees in exasperated innocence.

"Where is my good pen?" Bert's voice comes from the middle of the room, where he is tearing through a pile of papers on the table. How can anything be lost in a room measuring twelve by sixteen? I tell him he has twenty pens and they are all good. I tell him I am up here trying to read my book. There is a warning in my voice, which he misses or ignores.

An observer watching the humans settling in at Euphoria would see us too in an uneasy balance, would notice a pattern of approach and retreat, with frequent skirmishes over territory. Is it possible to have a private thought, a solitary moment? Bert seems to be everywhere. I look up from my book and he is there. When his chair scrapes the floor I start; when I lift a teacup he turns his head.

What we negotiate is small, several, and specific. Bert is an appropriator of space: he likes to spread out, to pile things up in an order not comprehended by lesser mortals. Astonished, I realize that he requires six feet of space in which to read a newspaper—arranging pages, coffee mug, glasses case, around him in imperial splendor. His movements are big, his voice is deep and resonant, he touches things as he passes. I become a defender of small regions, guarding my work area under the back window—a table-top measuring twenty-four by thirty inches—like sacred ground, but to no avail. The top bunk is my aerie, uncontested because undesired. I retreat there, leaving center stage, the floor below, to my expansive partner. Some afternoons I can hear him breathe.

"Listen to this," he calls up to me. "A man in Barnstable was arrested for hitting his girlfriend over the head with a twelve-inch statue of a cat. They're charging him with 'assault and battery with a deadly weapon.' But this woman in Hyannis hit her husband with a frying pan and they only called it 'a dangerous weapon.' Does that sound right to you?"

I let my breath escape with a subtle, hissing sound. "Yes," I say, "Yes. A frying pan sounds just right," and a new silence begins to vibrate from below.

These days Bert is off across the dunes before the mosquitoes and deerflies wake up. He carries strange equipment: a roll of reed, and sticks picked up along the beach, a knife, a camera, string, and a sketchpad. In his baseball cap, long pants and soft-soled shoes, reeking of musk and Deet, he's down in the bog this spring on his hands and knees, building a single, six-and-a-half-foot structure made of reed and driftwood branches that will preside among the cranberries and pines until fall.

When he drags himself back up the hill at midday, tired and very hungry, dripping sweat and bog water, he is preoccupied, full of himself, and wants to be waited on, to plunk himself down on the bunk and wearily accept food, sympathy, and back rubs. He enters grumbling, making guttural noises, and rearranging large pieces of furniture. Woe to the wife who doesn't look up from her notebook.

"I *just* need to finish this passage," I say, wadding up another wasted sheet of paper and aiming it toward the box on the floor.

"Why can't you go on and come back to it later?" he wants to know.

"Because I can't." The unsolved puzzle of a phrase leaves me paralyzed with frustration. I turn my back and let him know he has Interrupted Me.

Meanwhile, over the course of the morning, I have claimed all the space inside the shack, spreading papers across the table, half-read articles marked and propped on the bunk. Where is a guy supposed to stretch out anyway? He groans suggestively, sweeping the bottom bunk clear and pouring himself across it. It's Adam's curse, I tell him without sympathy: you live by the sweat of your face.

What's for lunch?

Thorns and thistles, bitter herbs.

So the quarrel begins, scripted in the ancient marriage code of never saying exactly what you mean. A wrong word, a quick heat followed by a coldness. This quarrel began because Bert moved some papers from the table and disturbed a very provisional order that was the holograph of a half-realized thought. He piled the papers up, as he thought, carefully, but in a manner which I interpreted as imperialistic. Talk quickly moves to weightier matters, concerning whether one of us has any consideration whatsoever for the other. I feel aggrieved and misunderstood. He works all morning without interruption, but expects me to drop everything when he walks in the door. He wants attention and care. He wants Donna Reed and he got Bertha Rochester.

For an alternate diversion I might point out my efforts during his absence: I hauled the water, swept the floor, made up the beds

. . . the list is pathetically short for eliciting sympathy, whoever did the work. It's hopeless, I think, as our argument unfolds. On a beautiful day, on a far and sandy shore, in the sweet wilderness together under a vast and arcing sky our voices rise and batter space. He asks when I am going to calm down and I tell him when hell freezes over.

There follows a silence during which I pretend to be working. Then Bert gets up, carefully, polite with antagonism. He says, "I'm just going to make some sausage and eggs, if that's all right with you."

He's looking straight at me. I can see his frustration and his anger, and I also see his love for me, which at the moment I probably do not deserve, and which he isn't dying to show me, but there it is. The way desire takes hold of us and lifts us and breaks us open so life can have its way. He picks up the knife and starts hacking at a roll of hard sausage.

"Be careful with that," I tell him.

"No," he says, smiling into my eyes, and my heart squeezes shut and skips a beat.

Our seclusion and the physical intimacies of the shack make us jittery as we settle in, too aware of one another, exaggerating the effect of every word or gesture. Perceptions sharpen: I feel seen at every turn, caught up in invisible strands of awareness.

The law of gravity states that bodies of similar mass will attract each other with a force inversely proportional to the distance between them. The closer the bodies, the greater the force. We warp space, deforming it; we fall toward one another like sleepers in a water bed. Impelled toward one another constantly, we live in imminent danger of collapse unless we pull apart by will, walk out in separate directions, bury our heads in books, or turn aside, asserting the independence of our separate selves. We create a balance between us, not by standing carefully in one spot, but by jostling, going too far and then retreating, until we know each other's ground entire.

For weeks I do not see my face. Euphoria has no mirrors except for the small steel plate Bert uses for shaving. Slowly the masks drop and our faces relax. Living side by side, we become again our unguarded selves, discovering the natural distance between one mind and another. We draw inward, not keeping all our emotions on the surface. Then, gradually the force of the speechless world around us begins to declare itself; its silence absorbs our excess and emotional static. In this calm the world speaks softly and draws us back; its quiet seeps through our skin and penetrates and we leave ourselves a little and expand to meet it.

The goldfinch is back on the weathervane, singing his heart out. He looks so bright and hopeful; what on earth is he thinking? "It's not too late," I want to tell him. "Look around you, see what's happening. Why do you want to get into it? Why not just skip it this year and have a peaceful life? It's summer, man, the seeds are ripening, life is sweet, why complicate everything?" But he wants it, there's no reasoning with him, so much bigger than he is that he doesn't know what to do with it. And pretty soon she'll come along and think it's all a great idea too.

Look at him there, the little hero, his head thrown back and his chest puffed with air. All imagination and vanity—you could say he's wasting his time—they'll be at each other's throats by August—but how can you, when he looks so pleased with himself, so bent on pulling all of life into him, on swallowing it whole, a world that's too big for him? We're too small; life pulls us and is breathed into us. It comes in a rush, this expanse of world claiming us. It breaks us, opens, and we rush toward it, against judgment and reason, and are swept and carried on its flow.

SEVEN

Mouse in House

Last night we could not sleep for hours, curiously restless, unable to settle into the dark folds of sheets and quilts. The dark, which came late, seemed to swallow us whole. I lay in the upper bunk, feeling the night with its unseen energies and the spaces within its silence, as I lay there like a radioactive element giving off consciousness in ticking half-lives. Bert grunted and thumped his pillow. An insect beat its wings against the screen, some sound that small, and the surf softly splashed below on the beach. Everything was in order, going about its business, night and day creatures in their places: the only thing out of order was us. Then there came a whisk and a scratching sound, like sand blown against wood, but more deliberate. It stopped, and started again, seeming loud. A mouse was scratching at the plug of tin foil we'd stuffed through the hole in the floor behind the bedpost, chewing, clawing, and nudging it upward. It stopped, started, stopped again. A silence, then something scurried across the floor and ran straight up the wall.

Bert, by virtue of having claimed the bottom bunk, is in charge of investigating all nighttime disturbances and so he got up, grabbed the flashlight, and lurched around in the dark, shining the light wildly in the corners and up the walls.

By the twitching yellow beam, the inside of the shack appeared in total disarray. It seemed impossible to make sense of space in that jabbing, irregular light. Suddenly objects would leap forward—odd, insane-appearing things—a lethal-looking can opener nailed to the wall, jaws open, gears unlocked—the thrust of a roof beam angled upward and swallowed into the dissolving dark. A brown boot lay on its side, split open like a gored animal. Bert stumbled and swore as a moth batted his ear and careened off, startling him so he hit his shin on the bench with a sickening thud. There was an ugly moment in which the bench stood in danger of reprisals, but the mouse ran across his foot at that minute, terrified, and the atmosphere softened. Bert caught him in the light and he froze and stared up at him. Tiny, no bigger than a thumb, but quivering with defiance—at the sight of him the war was over. Bert switched off the light and we heard the mouse scurry off in the welcome darkness. "You're outta here, pal," Bert laughed, then unbent and limped to the door, shooing the huge moth ahead of him with a grand sweeping motion. "You too. Everybody clear out." He stepped across the threshold, and stood there for a long moment.

"Cynthia, come here," he called quietly across the dark. I snaked down from the bed, found my footing and padded over to the door. The waves were turning over, shaping the edges of the land. Highland Light stroked the flanks of the dunes with its white beam. We stood together on the doorstep as a fleet of clouds moved out overhead, grandly opening the sky, and suddenly there were all the stars. The Big Dipper hung upside down, spilling into the northeast, with its two bright stars pointing to Polaris. The great dragon, Draco, high above the northern horizon, sprawled down into the western sky; in its tail is Thuban, the old North Star, by whose light the Egyptians aligned the pyramids. Far down at the southern horizon sat the Queen, Cassiopeia. For years now we have seen these stars above Euphoria, so clear and brilliant, each one familiar in its place, and the Milky Way opening overhead, with its shining dust trailing off, and still we can never believe it. An expanse, a universe with space enough in which to think or be anything.

We stood on the high deck facing into the dark as the wind blew us backward, westward, where night had gone. An off-shore wind was rising, and the deep, even pulsing of the waves beat up below on shore. The earth lay all dark and shadowless before us, darkness flooding the cool, still ground, black grasses standing motionless above black sand, alive in earth's night, and down below the water stretched itself out, gazing up at the sea of stars.

A meteor streaked down the sky, and as we leaned toward one another, I wished quickly for what I always wish: to be given another summer after this one, to be able to come here all our lives, to keep making this our home. In that quick flare I caught my breath, seeing it all race by, speed of light, our summer, our lives, and beyond that single spark only dark endless space. Looking into the sky's wide black expanse with its cold fire of stars, I come gratefully back to what is ours, this cloud-wrapped, spinning earth, these boards just holding back the wind. I wished for this very home, no more or less, but Bert's wish must have been more immediate, because he put his arms out and pulled me closer to him, urging me back inside, deep into the furthest corner of the shack and into his bed under the top bunk. There was just enough room there to sit up, all arms and legs in the little bunk, the headboard and footboard closing up the ends, one side pressed to the wall, the sheets mussed and warm, with grains of sand in their creases. Wrapped in long johns against the chill night, we unbandaged ourselves, goose-fleshed in the new air, cold, then warm, moisture glazing our skin. For once then, gravity was not a problem; with no distance between us, we agreed to the pull, to being drawn so close until our boundaries must have been indistinguishable, twining arms and legs, touching every-where, without a single worry about identity. Bone of my bones, and flesh of my flesh.

Whether the mouse left in peace or died on the spot from fear I don't know, but the night was quiet after that. The wind came up some hours later and I got up and pulled down extra blankets from the shelf. I spread one over Bert and he stretched gratefully in sleep and I hoisted myself back up into my own bunk. I slept until the sun rose in the window, hitting me in the eye, and then turned over to sleep again, hearing, faintly, the morning cries of the birds.

EIGHT

The Garden

I am sitting on the steps with my feet in the sand and I am trying to wake up. It's a brilliant morning: the sun just skims the hill, turning the grass tips all silver and blinking in the light. Down in the meadow, a squad of redwings cries and scatters upward, rattling the branches of the bayberry. Coffee breathes a thin vapor at the mug's rim; it curls and rises past my hands like a signal sent up in smoke.

The coffee is necessary. I wake these mornings in a daze, stupid, and barely able to recognize the world. Surfacing from the cold, deep currents of dream, where all things flow downward and melt into one story, I rise to meet the bright fact of daylight. Morning kills the dream, dissolving its images with light, chasing the shades of night back to their dark, unchanging underworld.

I dreamed I was taking an examination on the nature of time. I needed an answer I could write on the back of a maple leaf; the tree should have an answer hung from every leaf . . . Now I sit here, pulling at dream images, tugging them into the light, but they won't come. Deep-rooted, formless under the sun, they shred and tear apart like rotten seaweed. Already these memories are a story read long ago, dim as legend. Moments ago they were the air I breathed. I stand up, wipe my hands on my jeans, and start down the hill for water.

The pump groans and gushes, spurting water from the spigot and across the iron lip. Water splashes out, heavy and shining, over-flowing one bucket, then another, spilling onto the sand. A snake was here to drink before dawn, drawing S-shapes in the sand with his whole body. I fill four plastic jugs and set them in the bushes where the sun will heat them for our baths this afternoon. Then I refill the big basin we leave for priming and trudge uphill, the weight of water pulling my arms to earth. Bert is shoveling sand up around the exposed beams in back of the shack, in a futile campaign against the prevailing winds. He comes over to take the buckets from my hands, hoisting each one overhead on to the deck, and then turns back to his digging.

All summer we take turns scooping bites out of the backside of the dune, packing sand around the pilings as the hill moves off to the south. We buy time with our efforts, keeping a foothold as the dune slides out from under us. Each shovelful unearths layers of summers people have lived here, scrap from the constant building and rebuilding of the shack over forty years. We've turned up spoons and hinges, hundreds of rusty nails, a small green plastic soldier; these sift down to a certain substratum and surface again whenever the sand is moved, rising like bones into the light. Broken crockery, the spindles of a chair back tossed into the woodpile under the steps, glass, pennies, rusty twists of wire—the detritus of other lives floats just below the surface. This digging could go on forever and never stop uncovering objects; bones of ships lie buried in these dunes, their sails soft as parchment, spilled cargoes of rum, and dust of sailors. Our digging scatters particles of sand that shift and slide over one another, then shift back again. Ceaselessly, we shove the sand back as the dune slides out from under us. Ceaselessly, the wind undoes our work.

I climb the stairs and go inside, set the water buckets under the sink and cover them with tin plates, then take up the broom from behind the door. Our morning chores consist of sweeping, mak-ing up beds, sweeping, hauling water, washing up, and sweeping.

The wind pushes infinitesimal specks through the cracks all night, piling up ridges of finest dust at every opening. Grains of sand are carried in our clothes, stuck to our skin. There's sand in the bed-covers, sand in the grooves of the driftwood table, sand filtering down from the unfinished ceiling. I sweep beneath the stove, under the table, and scoot the sand across the doorstep. I figure I move a quart of sand a day, a volunteer in the war against entropy.

Sweeping the old, soft boards, brushing pale sand across sun-gold wood, light flashes up through a crack in the floorboards, and for a moment I remember dreaming. Flowers on a bare, rotted limb, a huge bird gulping down a frog . . . The light beyond these four walls opens into a wide and endless space; the image flees into the dazzling fullness beyond, and then the whisper of broom straw shushes thought. I pull the bedsheets tight, smoothing out creases to obliterate the landscape created in a night. The red covers tuck tight into the wooden bedframes, and fat white pillows loll against the headboards as if nothing had ever happened here.

The screen door bangs shut. Reaching up to pin damp towels on the line, I feel a quick breeze whip them out of my arms. The towels thrup, tugging at the cord as wind fills them; the line strains and then goes slack. In a wash of color, the dream stains the air. Blue smoke rising, an odor of onions along a dim hallway. These are not images of the mind. They seem not to belong to me at all, but to be effigies of another, wilder, world, one I can barely recognize, though it seems to know me well.

A blue house shining from a hundred windows. I walked up the stairs and through the door, knowing my way though I had never been there before, though in fact this house does not exist. I walked into a room and met my father at the stove frying peacock's eggs—I did not say to him, *oh, you are dead*, because it was a dream.

A girl with no legs was being lowered by ropes into a pond beside a country road. She bobbed high in the water like a cork, smiling and waving, and after a while they fished her out with a hook.

Why not believe it? I saw these things, smelled food cooking, felt the warm mist bead up on my skin. Behind closed eyes my brain filled with light, and images that made my eyes jerk back and forth, chasing phantoms. Lying still, I felt myself running down city streets; I climbed long staircases that opened into fields of wildflowers.

These creations appear and melt away. Then follows imperial morning, the light succeeds, and I wake to this world and believe it equally.

I work at making a home here, imagining and building it, like a sketch of a life in this single room, one board thick, but my dreams insist I have another life, and no home here that matters. Between this side and the other one there is no easy connection: every night the rules get changed and this world blows away; the wind whisks dust of sand through my sleep, erasing everything I know, thrusting me down a dark corridor that spills me out, spinning, into deep space.

With our daily routines we reinforce an order, but my true mind knows there is no time, no space, no cause or effect, no beginning or end, and everything I call my own has been created out of whole cloth, all illusion. I work at making a marriage, letting eros lead me past fear, learning partnership and simple liking, living side by side—but in sleep I inhabit a solitary kingdom. Try telling your dreams to another person and that gulf appears. You find yourself on another shore wildly waving, shouting, repeating yourself, as your listener's eyes glaze over.

The steps creak underfoot; I stand at the door and my shadow falls on the floor in front of me. Light streams through the windows, washing the stained sink, the dented aluminum kettle, the scarred counters and tabletop, in a glow so intensely revealing it seems to glorify whatever it touches. In this moist air each object stands apart from its surroundings, haloed in reflected light. Molecules of water suspended in the air make every surface shimmer; colors are deep, saturated. The world shines, acutely particular, with cracks of use: a blotch of rust etched into old porcelain, the dull, reverberating whiteness of a china plate, littered with golden crumbs. Steam curls from the lip of the kettle, which holds, reflects, absorbs light in its battered surfaces, and I pour out a mug of hot, sweet, milky tea for Bert, drain the last of the coffee into my cup, and call him to come and take a break.

He appears around the back corner of the shack in jeans and a white t-shirt, the shovel gripped upright, looking like a true son of the working class. "Hold out your hand," he tells me, smiling, and places something cool and hard in my palm. It's a huge blue-glass marble, almost as big as a ripe plum. Its surface has been scratched and pitted by sand. "It was buried in the side of the dune: look, you can see the sky in it," he says. "It's like one of those mirror balls people put in their gardens." I hold it up—a fish-eye bending light into itself so the whole sphere of this world collapses into one small, scarred blue globe. A shaft of sunlight flashes deep within its blue heart, revealing a swirl of motion where the ground arches up to meet the sky's dome.

As I look in, seeing how the grass and clouds are now touching one another, a deeper reflection swims to the surface, growing slowly sharper, like an image in a crystal ball. "Look," I tell him, bending closer, "We're in there too." Small and distant, our faces peer up as if from underwater. We lean our heads close and gaze back at ourselves floating below the sky.

We sit on the bottom step together, looking out across a scene we love. The view before us is of a nearly empty world—sky, sand, and water reflecting light from all their surfaces, holding no image between them. But in this austere, mineral world are scattered patches of green. Grasses wave their heads on a breeze, their leaves opening and closing, roots holding on to bare sand. The dark knot of the bayberry, seven stories of branches crossing in air, casts its shadow network on the ground, and the dusty miller thrusts itself upward in woolly clumps. Roses open to the sun, perishable and many-folded, with dark, complicated petals. Bert rests his hand on the back of my neck, and begins kneading the muscles along the top of my shoulders. I breathe in his clean, sweaty, man smell, taste his breath that smells like tea. The marble sits in my palm, heavy, round, compressing a world that moves when this one does, layer on layer of light folding images in its surfaces. This day I entered so slowly now wraps me like another kind of dream, a mirage of light and bird song, of sand-colored grasshoppers that feed at the grassroot, green leaves and little yellow flowers. A dream the dreamer will believe fully for a while, however long it lasts.

I could write time on the back of a leaf. The leaf opens and drinks in light, pulls water up from the root, breathes oxygen into the air. Pulling up dream water, the leaf unfurls; it withers and falls, then again it swells and opens. We breathe that light gladly; we eat the food of time. That same sun that split the clouds at dawn, whose early heat sent me down the hill for water, shines past this earth continually, knowing neither night nor day, a star burning in the bluest reaches of space where we hang suspended, tangled in a web of leaves and branches, peering out at a changing sky.

NINE

❧

Beach Rights

Down on the beach the terns are crying, convinced that every shadow threatens their eggs. The bare-swept beach infuriates them; with no refuge from sun or tides, they are exposed, seeing everything, seen constantly. Again and again, they rise off their nests to attack the sky with trembly wings, and subside uneasily. When the marsh hawk sails overhead they scream in outrage, mobbing her until she wheels out of sight.

The sun has been up for hours. A white haze hangs over the water, and heat currents rise along shore, shimmering the air. Tangled lumps of rockweed and matted sea lettuce festoon the upper beach, sending up a rank odor of salt and vegetable rot as the sun broils them.

We found four dead kittiwakes on the beach this morning, spread out at intervals over a mile and a half: pretty little birds, a species of arctic gull, white and pale grey, with sharp black wing tips. They've wandered far out of their normal range to come here. They should be up by the Gulf of St. Lawrence or beyond, nesting on cliffs above a rocky coast. They're off course by a thousand miles, give or take a few hundred. Russ Wilson, one of the rangers, came down the beach in his jeep as we stood puzzling over one of the bodies. He told us the kittiwakes have been dying of a fungus infection: park rangers have found more than a hundred dead ones along the back shore. Perhaps the climate here is not healthy for them, or they were sick already and that took them off course. Either way, it's the wrong place, wrong time.

The beach is a livelier place these days, peopled by several contentious tribes. Sanderlings run back and forth with the waves, scuttling along the surf line with what one of my guidebooks calls "pathological dedication." Then a score of them will take flight, wheeling off at our approach, like a flower opening in midair. We saw a piping plover scooting along in the jeep tracks, pecking into wrack and seaweed, disappearing and then popping back into view. Sparrow-sized, all grey and white except for his black collar and yellow legs, he appeared determined, in a small way, modest but unyielding, but what he was about I didn't gather. Probably looking for sea worms or fly larvae, for which I wish him all the luck.

Whales have been spouting offshore all week: finbacks playing in the waves, sometimes five or six of them together at once. Yesterday we watched them for more than an hour until a fishing boat cut in close to shore and they took off for deeper waters. They swim to the surface, spout, and dive, showing a flash of fin or tail as they fold their enormous bulky selves back into the water; sometimes they seem to float on the surface, gently rolling over and back. Even at several hundred yards offshore, their playfulness is obvious, that huge, lively buoyancy and energy. Where do they come from, what world, which quadrant, that they should be here with us on an ordinary day, whole families of them at ease? Stormy Mayo, from the Center for Coastal Studies, said he's never seen so many here before: the whale watch boats go out from Provincetown and the whales swim out to meet them, swimming right up to the sides. From Long Point to High Head, people are seeing schools of finbacks, a bounty of finbacks, and nobody bothers them at all.

By early June the terns have established their colonies along the back shore. They return every spring from South America to nest here, where the offshore bars offer good fishing and the unbroken beach suits their exacting standards for privacy. All day we glimpse them at the edge of our vision, in constant motion, hovering over the water with fast, shallow wingbeats, constantly crying as they circle and swoop over the shallows, then fold their wings to plunge headfirst into the water to seize a sand eel or a minnow.

The terns are birds of air and sea, excitable and nervous, unhappy on land. Maintaining a fragile balance at the edge of the tides, their existence is hazardous at best, and never more so than when they are nesting. They seem to know this and take it to heart, violently protesting any intrusion into their territory. Their nests are mere depressions scratched out above the tideline, offering no protection from storms or predators. An ocean storm at high tide can wipe them out. Their eggs look like small pebbles, and the chicks, when they hatch, are tiny, the color of dry sand, and given to hiding in wheel ruts for shade on hot afternoons, where they are liable to get run over.

This year they have settled a little to the east of Snail Road, down toward Thalassa. We're just as glad to have them at a distance. The past two summers they nested right in front of Euphoria, and we had to cut a wide detour behind them in order to reach the water. Still, they would fly up in outrage every time we appeared on the crest of the hill, and charge straight at us, screeching. As we headed down the beach, the birds followed us, scolding and fluttering overhead; often one, then another, would climb high into the air and turn to rush at the highest point, which happened to be our heads, swooping twenty feet or more before shearing off just short of scalp hair.

Their anger was so exorbitant we had to constantly remind ourselves of our good will—we were not out to steal eggs or chicks, or even to walk any closer to the nests than we could possibly help. I wished them well, I told myself, as cries of murder rang in the air. Still, some smallness in me wanted to cry back at all their crying, at its endlessness, its uncompromising insistence that everything done here pertains to them. Do they own the beach? It seems they cannot rest with less. They fly back and forth over the water and the bare swept sand, saying over and over that we are detested, that our mere being here threatens them, that it does no good to mean well, that there is no meaning well that matters except to disappear from here entirely.

Now that there are eggs, the park rangers have roped off the tern's colony and posted signs to keep off traffic. Rangers come by twice a day now to count the eggs and assess their progress, an attention the birds appear to appreciate not in the least, judging by all the clamor. When the chicks begin to hatch out, the beach will be closed to vehicles. This always provokes a lot of outrage on the part of fishermen and other off-road vehicle owners, and rekindles the usual debate in the local paper about beach rights and public access, an argument based on the assumption that no place on earth can be called accessible unless you can drive to it.

When the chicks begin to hatch, the parents grow more belligerent than ever, quarreling among themselves and chasing every other creature from the nesting area. Gulls fly over the nests, chuckling, seemingly oblivious to the discord, and are harried along by the outraged terns. The arrival of the marsh hawk upon the dune ridge sends them into a state of hysteria. We watch from a distance, sometimes with field glasses. At high noon they're up when they should be down, most nervous when the sun is high. I'm imagining fried eggs, and no wonder, but they settle back only to fly up again, twisting in the air, small angry knots of protesting creation.

We watch them, wheeling in their tight dives, zigzagging erratically over the shallows. However high-keyed and even irrational their dispositions, the birds themselves are a wonder. They are all subtle response, exquisite, instinctive followers of currents. Over and over they rise off their nests to attack the sky with trembly wings and subside, and rise again. Delicate and graceful, ardent and bright, they circle tirelessly over the water and back, searching for fish. From beneath, their bright white bellies gleam against the sky; then they fold their wings and dive, plunging head first into the waves and pulling up at the last second to graze the surface of the water, emerging with a shiny silver sand eel dangling from their beaks.

Where have they come from, these terns, these ill-fated kittiwakes, these finbacks and plovers, and the sanderlings who scan the water's edge so anxiously? What currents have they followed to find this shore? It's the season when migrants come to stay, when claims are pressed, the sensitive business of raising the young in an uncertain world, but we see only an arc of their circle, only a moment of their lives grazing ours. They come from north and south, following ocean currents and star trails, the crests of mountain ranges and tug of the earth's magnetic field; they come here to begin their tribe again, and then they are off on further journeys. Where is their home but wherever they are?

The terns arrive from South America after flights of a thousand miles. It seems outrageous, on the face of it, for them to come here and pick out a piece of territory and drive everyone else away. The claims of these migratory species ask us to redefine, or expand, our notion of home. We are accustomed, once we get past the purely legal matter of property rights and monied interests, to define home ground as something validated by time as well as space; a history of habitation, cultivation, in a particular spot seems to justify a deeper claim. But these seabirds appear out of the sky, on one arc of a voyage compassing thousands of miles, and lay claim to whatever stretch of beach best suits their needs, an utterly practical attachment which ends as soon as the need for it ends. They come from far away, on the arcs of great circles, but they belong here, if only for a little while, because they need to be here. To put against all odds, the terns have only their extraordinary vehemence, their persistence, and those incessant, high-pitched cries. Yes, they do own the beach. And when we enter their space, with or without design, they fly at us out of the sky, crying accusation. They are right: they want to live.

TEN

※

Beach Roses

We're knee-deep in June, June for Juno, queen of heaven and goddess of fertility. Now leafy shadows cover the bare earth; bees hum in the unfurling blossoms of beach pea and rose. In the woods along the highway, on hillsides above Pilgrim Lake and at High Head, the shadbushes raise white showers of petals into the air, and birds gobble the berries down their throats. It's spring in full throttle, at high tide, coming to a head, getting up speed, and busting out all over. Big breaths of it fill us with invisible flower particles that fly out again in swirls. The fire in the sky gets into our veins and makes our hearts go fast as hummingbirds', splurging life energy.

Flying toward the solstice, we rise into that meeting with light. Within a few days everything north of the arctic circle will be bathed in twenty-four hours of sunlight. Here we're getting about fourteen hours, a minute or so more every day, pure energy from a star, burning down on us, quickening the life within a seed, an egg, a stony planet.

Spend, breathe, burn. All this excitement makes me hungry. I sat down at the table and devoured a huge meal before heading out this morning: thick brown bread topped with baked beans, a fried egg, and ketchup, all washed down with strong black coffee—what I call cowboy breakfast. Bert looks at my plate and shudders.

On my morning tour, a morning when nothing is happening except what always happens, when footprints made in the night by wild, free-living creatures appear fresh and new, and green things poke themselves up out of the sand as if for the first time, the world seems lucid, nearly intelligible. It's a day as clear as any in creation, seeming like the beginning of the world, which it is. Adam and Eve would recognize this limpid light, and wish they could start all over. Down by the pump, beach roses crowd the path in their first bloom, sending up a scent so sweet and lush it almost has weight on my tongue. Beach peas swell modestly inside their pale green pods, and the seaside goldenrod forms tight nubs of blossom along its stems.

The path curls up past the pump, around and down again, into a blowout where the wind has scooped out a circle of hard sand behind the first dune. This is the beach of about 1934, closed in by building sand: nothing grows here; the sand is packed hard, and raw, salty winds blow across the top of the dune, alive with old sea smells. Two big metal hulks, parts of a ship's boiler that washed up years ago, sit rusting in the sun, their pocked, burnt-orange hulls taken up, molecule by molecule, into the air. Hollow, big enough for a child to stand up inside, with square holes cut out of their sides, they squat on the sand, silently burning, and seem to watch me as I pass.

Crossing Snail Road, I double back inland along the vehicle track kept open by Art's Dune Tours. The track runs parallel to shore behind the outermost line of dunes. Sheltered in this valley, there is a profusion of green these days. Woody shrubs of bayberry, rose, and beach plum form little thickets on the lee slope, and along the marsh floor meadowsweet, steepletop, and sheep laurel rise to audacious heights of two or three feet, launching themselves into space. To my right, along the slope of the second dune, bearberry spreads an evergreen carpet across the sand. Lichens and poverty grass form little mounds, and the warm dusty scent of the pitch pines lifts up out of the valley.

And here, loveliest of all, sprawled across the path, its flowers full and heavy on the branches, all flushed and sweet and pink as dawn, appears the resident genius of the place, *Rosa rugosa*. *Rosa rugosa* means "wrinkled rose"—the flower is also called salt spray rose, wild rose, dune rose, seaside rose. With its flat, silky blossoms, shaggy yellow centers, and dark green leaflets as creased and soft as washed cotton, it is our local beauty. The rugosa blooms straight through from June into September. At once hardy and sweet, growing right up out of the sand, no other flower seems so much an emblem of this place. It grows in salt air, in poor soil and harsh winds, fastening itself to the land as if these conditions were what made it. Yet in fact, the beach rose is an immigrant, a piece of flotsam, no less than those metal hulks that lie staring on the sand. A shipwreck flower from the Orient, its seeds washed up on shore from some capsized Japanese freighter or fishing boat, took root and learned to flourish here and then to thrive. So still, an emblem of the place.

In June you can feel the full shock it must have been to see the first flower wither. Everything is growth, budding, opening into light. It seems this must be the way of the world, a blossoming with no cost, the magical light thrusting through the plants, shifting the ground, beginning over and over.

Everywhere I look I see the rebirth of roses, new grasses waking in clusters of yellow, wind-shredded spears, the berry hugged in the root of the blossom. Last year all the roses died, and their petals blew across the sand. But this spring the world fills with roses again, and little moist leaves folded tight against the stems. At the base of every rose are a thousand roses, buried in the rosehip, the seedpod. So that if all the roses were gone but one, only one rose remaining, we would still have roses. And so for goldenrod, cranberry, huckleberry and pine, all flowers in a single flower, eternal repetitions of life appearing in succession, even as the petals fly to the ground.

The track curves around and sinks deep in sand, a green corridor shaded by miniature oaks and pine. Just over the hill is the densest cluster of shacks at Peaked Hill: Boris Margo's, Harry Kemp's, Grace Bessay's, the Hunzingers'. A footpath winding through high grass, and a pump half hidden in bushes, are all I can see from here. Off to the right the low roof of Jim Bowen's decrepit shack folds itself into an encroaching dune.

Further on, the old Coast Guard boathouse lies collapsing beside the road. It was abandoned here half a century ago when the Coast Guard moved its operations into town. Open at both ends, the boathouse lies swamped in goldenrod, the sun streaming in through gaping holes in its shingles. A sand dune is building up inside against the far wall, shouldering its way between the boards, and the hard sand in front glitters with chips of glass from parties that ended thirty years ago, when the boathouse was still standing. Now, with its floorboards heaved up in splinters, its walls buckled in, it looks like a single step could bring it down.

Resting atop its own rubble, buried in leaves and vines, and leaned on by a moving sand dune, the boathouse lies three hundred yards from the beach, in a quiet of stopped wind. Nearby sits the concrete foundation of the old Life Saving Station, built here after the two stations before it slid into the waves. A strange hush hangs over the place. Even the incessant voice of the waves is stopped in this narrow valley. The little, blue-black tree swallows have it now: their soft twittering cries run before them as they dart among the shadows, over broken boards and ivy. A brown snake slides quietly up the listing wall and slips under the leaves.

I always feel a chill as I approach this spot, haunted by birds and deerflies. How tenuous our hold here seems, even in this green valley shining in sunlight, even on such a bright spring morning. I look at the boathouse covered in vines, its interior filling up with sand, and I feel my life slipping away under me, the sand blowing over, covering everything I know. It buries living plants, erases each familiar shape of hill and coastline. Sand fills in the hollows of our houses and then leaves cover the sand. Mice scramble under the floorboards, and sparrows play along the roof. The sand blows and moves and makes a new world, tunneled by ants. What persists? A spoon, a splinter of glass, a toy soldier risen up from the wreckage. A blue-green marble reflecting the sky. We live on top of other lives, pulling water up from old wells, moving on as the sea takes the land away, but we can never know for sure where our place is in the succession. A house of boards declining inch by inch into the earth, sunlight dappled through a broken roof, the bright eyes of swallows in the leaves. And the brown snake, sliding quietly up the leaning wall: egg robber, destroyer of nests—his place is here too. I would have followed him if I could, into that dim and dusty place, back into the lost garden, closed to me. Instead I turn aside and begin to climb the hill. There's a pump half-hidden in the brush, I know where, with a tin cup hanging from the handle by a string, and a path leading up to a shack. Nobody lives there now, but there are birdhouses nailed up on posts around the doorstep, with swallows swooping and crying all around. Roses grow by the doorstep, and from that doorstep you can see for a very long way.

ELEVEN

Jacob's Ladder

One day last summer I found a man sleeping in the dunes. It was late morning and I was out for blueberries, climbing the side of a dune to get to a meadow on the other side. Halfway up the slope the path began to curve inward, and I followed it until it became overgrown with poison ivy. Hesitating, I looked around, then chose a steeper, winding route, avoiding the laces of the vines, and finally came out on to a little clearing of dune grass and bearberry, its sandy floor studded by dark scat of rabbits.

Sunlight splashed the bright leaves of the ivy. Sprays of meadowsweet rose up below, wavering on their long stems, and the little yellow blossoms of the poverty grass winked among the low green. Moving forward, I saw there below me at the bottom of the dune a form stretched flat, not moving. For a terrible moment I thought he was dead. But the man, the stranger, was sleeping, tucked up in a sleeping bag, curled on his side. He had rolled himself up close to the edge of a dune, on a bare patch of sand ringed by trees and a thicket of scrub oak, hidden from view of anyone passing, except from this exact, unlikely spot. I pulled back quickly, then crept up to look again. He lay in deep sleep, his chest and shoulders half out of the army blanket. He was wearing a black t-shirt and looked like a giant slug or a larva in its chrysalis. Only in sleep he was already the butterfly, orange and black winged.

I stood there without breathing, afraid to turn. Partly it was my normal fear of meeting a stranger in the open, any woman's fear of the hobo, the man among the brush. There is a danger in the woods, in isolated places; thinking of it spoils everything, but it's there just the same. At the same time there was something uncanny in the man's presence. He had an air of integrity, a self-possession in the midst of utmost vulnerability. He was not, at this moment, his usual self, but a traveler outside time and space. Watching his chest rise and fall, I felt I was trespassing on some deep privacy. His face was clear of any expression except for rapt attention, as if he were dreaming hard, studying the dark for clues. His black hair stood up from his forehead like a brush, giving him a surprised look. I leaned over, wondering, trying to read his expression like a code, but the vision was closed to me, belonging to another world.

He might have been some hiker or traveler out of money for a room, or perhaps just someone who wanted to spend a night out here. Camping in the dunes is not allowed—he knew enough to choose a place hidden from the jeep paths, out of rangers' eyesight. This sleeping in the dunes was an old town tradition before the Park Service came. A fight in a bar or an argument at home sent many men out here to sleep off their liquor or their rage. It was a great free place, a place of open space and mental scope, against the backside of the small, all-seeing town where everyone knew your life. This sleeper might have been a townsman, or a runaway, but then he might as well have been a god, surprised among the morning's bright leaves.

He blew out a sharp breath and turned over abruptly and I startled and froze, but he did not waken. We might have frightened each other thoroughly then, but instead he turned and snuffled down into deeper sleep. I backed slowly down the path, barely breathing until I was some distance from where he lay. I left the sleeper sleeping, a free man with no life, and gave up my idea of blueberries for that day. Meanwhile, my traveler lay in his body and watched the galaxies turn.

Jacob lay out under the stars and dreamed a ladder to heaven, with angels going up and down, and God promised him the land where he lay and he called the place the gate of heaven. In the dream we are gods, graciously descended into the world. But we wake and the stairway has vanished, the connection is broken. Still, we erect a heap of stones to remember the place where we met ourselves ascending and descending.

In the shack, I dream the shack, reconstructing it board by board. I dream the real, igniting cells that blossom over and over in my mind, saying: "rose, snake, rabbit." You nose around the fenceposts, sniff the air and leave prints in the sand. You nibble a leaf. You put your head under your wing and blink toward sleep. You close white petals at twilight, feel the spears of your leaves furled against the wind, holding in warmth and moisture. You are sand, many-faceted, your molecules arranged in crystal firmaments, surrounding eons of empty space. You are empty space, ready to ignite with a word. You see a snail cross the sand and hesitate. An angel sleeps in the garden, guarding the portal. A man in a black t-shirt, rolled up in a blanket, walks among stars.

The stranger sleeps at the foot of the dune and space stands back around him. He cannot see himself or me; I feel his breath a hundred yards off, and after I turn and walk away, I watch him with my mind.

TWELVE

※

A Visit to Zena's

We're reading in our bunks after lunch when a voice sings out "Hello!" and footsteps bang up the stairs. It's Annie, our neighbor from town, peering in through the screen, her blonde braids glinting in the sun. We call come in and she does, bringing three cold beers—magnificent green bottles sweating beads of chill. No, she doesn't want one; we put them away for later.

Annie looks appraisingly around the shack, the way people do who have stayed here before, alert and suspicious of possible changes. She lived in Euphoria one summer when her daughter Phoebe was a baby. (I've always meant to ask what she did for diapers out here, but I suppose Phoebe just went without.) She's come to invite us over to the Bowen shack for wine and cake after supper. It's Phoebe's seventh birthday, and they're spending the night, along with Gabriella and her daughter Lulu.

If anyone could merit the label "dune rat," it would be Annie. She has been coming here since she was a teenager and has stayed in just about every shack on the back shore, including a lot of time in Thalassa. Several years ago, though, she and Hazel had a falling out—Annie says it was over a beach party that got the attention of the park rangers—and since then she's stayed in Frenchie's shack and at Bowen's, but never in either of Hazel's shacks. We suspect, too, that Annie's ways were a little too relaxed for Hazel's liking.

Jim Bowen's shack doesn't really belong to Jim Bowen, but he's the latest caretaker. It belongs to Vic Peters's sister, Zena, but she doesn't use it anymore. It's a peculiar structure, built low and far back in the dunes, sunken among pines, and is used by a fairly casual assortment of people, most of whom at least profess to know Jim Bowen. It's the crash pad of the dunes, never locked, seldom repaired, and it seems to be gently declining back into the earth from whence it came.

We agreed to come over after supper and then we all talked a bit. Annie didn't have much news. A steady sort of person, she lacks the kind of appetite for gossip which would attract the finer particles of rumor and supposition which circulate in this town. Still, she'd know if someone had died or gotten divorced, or if there was a major fire, so it was worth checking in to be sure.

She couldn't stay. Gabriella had packed a lunch and was meeting her on the beach with the children. We wandered out onto the deck without quite saying goodbye, our talk trailing off. The afternoon was warm and clear, the big dome of sky settling over the last line of dunes to the west, and along the clean horizon of the ocean. A song sparrow flitted busily in the bayberry just below us, and then the cock pheasant crowed from the high grasses, his voice seeming to scrape the air. He's been around this past week at all hours; he preens and stamps his feet, then lets loose a strangled love cry, hoping to attract a female. So far he's had no luck that we can tell.

Annie disappeared down the path by the pump as we watched. In the distance, we could see someone over at Boris Margo's shack, walking back and forth around the door and windows. The shack has been boarded up since last July; we wondered whether Boris's nephew had come at last. The figure seemed to be moving deliberately; he was carrying something—tools? lumber?—it was hard to tell at such a distance. He stopped to examine the window frame and the shingles around the door. We wondered whether it was a trespasser trying to get inside, and then

Bert spotted a blue truck pulled up the track, along the inland road that only locals use, and so it was all right.

The pheasant crowed again, and strutted into the open. He threw back his head and began marching up and down on the hard sand, his chest thrust forward, swinging his long, pointed tail around with each turn. His wings glinted in the sun; his brilliant green head and red eye patch vibrated with color; he was magnificent, princely, master of all before him, and then he beat his wings, lifted his head, and let out that unfortunate cry. A cackle, a gargle, a screech. All space stood back, embarrassed.

Eight o'clock, Bowen's, the sky still blue with light. A fire on the ground outside the shack had gone out, leaving a ring of charred wood and blackened sand surrounded by corn husks, sticks for roasting things, the remains of dinner. Phoebe and Lulu were out in front on the trampled sand, both of them sun-browned and dirty and in a dissident mood. They presented a contrast: Phoebe at seven, tall and blonde, all legs and arms, and three-year-old Lulu squat and brown, with dark hair cut short like a boy's, gold-bead earrings, black eyes of a warrior. A day of sun and sea air had honed their dispositions to a defiant edge. As we approached, Phoebe was rhythmically pounding a stick on the hard sand, chanting, "I want . . . another corn . . . I want . . . another corn," which was evidently not forthcoming, though judging from the remains strewn about they had gone through a dozen ears already. "I want . . . another corn." Lulu stood watching her, deeply fascinated, her black eyes fixed on Phoebe's every move. Phoebe might have been doing this a long time because the refrain had lost whatever urgency it might have had and seemed to be fluctuating between complaint and some sort of tribal chant. If she had begun in anger, her temper had subsided and she now seemed to be in the process of hypnotizing herself, and Lulu, with the repetition.

Lulu did not acknowledge our approach by so much as a breath or a spark of movement, but Phoebe hooded her eyes and turned partially aside to ignore our greeting. The two of them there, in front of the blackened fire in the evening light, seemed to inhabit a separate world, sealed off from us by a thin barrier of will. I could feel the combination of tiredness, petulance, and boredom driving the girls, the scary pull of their wildness, and so I let it be and went by quietly. Another minute and we'd all be leading some sort of sacrifice.

You enter Bowen's shack by ducking through a small anteroom, just an enclosed doorway without windows, like entering a cave. A hand-lettered sign on the door reads: "This door is not locked, so please don't break it down." Inside, the shack is square and low, with windows reaching down to the ground. (Actually, the sand has piled up to the windows.) The place has a sort of hippie squalor and coziness—a worn rug on the floor, one window with no glass in it, shaded by an Indian print curtain, a sagging double bed in the corner, and in the center of the room, a big table ringed with half a dozen mismatched chairs in various states of disrepair. If Euphoria's interior has the elegant simplicity of a boat, Bowen's is a sixties dorm room.

Annie and Gabriella had finished cleaning up the supper things, and had already started in on the wine. Gabriella was speaking excitedly in her heavy Paris accent, making vehement gestures in the air as she exclaimed over some affront. She noticed us, and without pausing waved, "Come in," and kept talking.

Chairs were shoved and switched around, to find the ones least likely to break under us, and soon we were seated at the table, sipping wine. It seemed Gabriella was infuriated over a run-in that afternoon with the Hunzingers, who have a shack down past Thalassa on the inner side of the dune. They had stormed out of their shack to chase the children off the dune ridge, yelling incoherently about their "property"—Roy Hunzinger shouting and waving his fist in the air as he chased the women and girls away while Mrs. Hunzinger stood behind him, stolid and unyielding, holding the second line of defense. Gabriella was indignant: "They think they own the whole place?" she demanded, slapping her hand against the table.

"The Grouches," Annie said wryly, applying the children's term for them. "Oscar and Grungetta."

That sort of incident is nothing new. For years everyone here has kept a wary distance from the Hunzingers, whose tempers are notorious. They are the mean old couple in every neighborhood: the man who yells about his lawn, the old woman who calls the police about street noise at ten p.m. See them peering out through curtains, bristling with suspicion, always on guard against some unspecified threat. People who don't like kids or dogs, who view every approach as an intrusion. What are they doing here, we wonder, and concede bewilderment. Nobody has ever seen them walk beyond their own fence, much less glimpsed them on the beach. They've made a compound of their place, a half acre of bare sand ringed with barbed wire, and flood lights aimed at the perimeter. Their cabin has two rooms, a porch, and is painted a forbidding, military shade of green. A generator runs the lights and powers an electric pump, a water heater, and a television. Every Friday during the summer they drive over the big dune in their old white pickup, staring ahead with fixed gazes, gun it up-hill and down, straight through the barbed wire gate, then for all anybody can tell, they sit in front of the television all weekend and drink. On Monday they return to New Hampshire.

"Why can't they drink in New Hampshire?" Gabriella wanted to know.

Gabriella was saying something should be done. Enough was enough. Someone should confront them, set them straight. Bert disagreed. "Not in a million years! Leave them alone." He pressed the point. "That's just the kind of person who goes off and pulls a gun. Think about it. Every night on the news you hear it, some-body goes too far. And the neighbors say, 'Well we thought he was a little strange, but we never believed he'd do anything like that.' Leave the crazy assholes alone, both of them. They never go past their fence, so do the same. Just keep away and stay out of it."

"Mmm . . ." Annie was making little harmonizing noises, sipping her wine. It was hard to tell whether she agreed, or had moved off into another zone of thought. Annie and Gabriella are great friends, women who are raising their daughters alone and trying to take life as they find it. They are more relaxed about this than I could ever be, patient, and glad of small pleasures, managing to regard their children with constant affection and reasonable pride. Otherwise, they could not be more different. Gabriella is fiery, impatient, small and muscular, with a French passion for justice and political philosophy. Annie is calm, practical, inclined to take the world as it is.

I could feel the red wine spreading warmth down my limbs, bringing heavy relaxation after another day of sun. The talk moved on to other subjects and Gabriella began to calm down, having had her say. Maybe the wine was working on all of us. I felt it in my muscles first, sinking into the chair, my arm leaned on the table, the relaxation gradually spreading upward into my brain and tongue. Annie told of her talk that afternoon with Dennis Minsky, the tern warden. A great horned owl has been preying on the colony at High Head, wiping out over half of the chicks so far. Dennis goes down every morning to count, and every morning more chicks are gone. We said it was a shame, but what could you do? Owls, hawks, foxes, they've all been here forever. It's nobody's fault, we agreed. Than Annie called the girls in, got them to wash up after a fashion, and began slicing the cake. Phoebe was not interested in discussing her birthday. "Don't sing," she begged. The cake—a carrot cake—was sweet, heavy, and tasted overly nutritious. The girls sat at the far corner of the table, chewing with what I took for resentment until I realized they were practically falling asleep. Soon they were rolled into the corner where a foam mattress was laid out with an open sleeping bag over it, and a flannel sheet was spread over their unmoving bodies.

As the sun finished going down a few mosquitoes floated in through the open window. It got darker and cooler, and the mosquitoes went away. Bowen's doesn't have lamps, or propane for that matter—there's too much danger of fire the way people come and go here. A battery-powered camplight on the table gave a weak yellow glow, and Annie had unpacked a candle stub whose flame glinted in a blue jar. In the dusk, talking softly now as the girls plummeted toward sleep, we heard the soft sounds of evening around us. Sand moving across sand, a gull crying overhead.

There began to be more light outside than in the room. It is the most private hour, this moment of twilight when inside and outside blend. The shadows gathering in the corners seem sheltering, safe. Nothing will come to us here, I thought. A fork scraped a plate, and on the other side of the hill a jeep gunned its engine in soft sand. Bert stood up and walked to the cupboard, filled a glass with water from a jug and drank it down. I watched his strong, confident movements. Would Roy Hunzinger really get a gun? It didn't seem possible. The cock pheasant called from the far hill. Once, then twice again, nearer. He must be working this side of the woods as well. He keeps a large territory during mating season, nesting with several females at once, going from nest to nest. His cry was urgent, choked with need, and we laughed uneasily in its aftermath, embarrassed by its vulgar, ungainly desire.

Conversation halted, then resumed more slowly. The girls turned in their sleep, murmuring, shadows settled deeper in the corners of the shack and then the pheasant screamed, right under the window, and splintered the quiet. We all started and jerked our heads around. A flutter passed across the room, and then he screamed again, and our faces closed. Annie yawned and tipped the wine bottle over her glass, dribbling a last half inch of dusky red. Time to go.

We walked home in the ashy light, the little toads hopping away ahead of us in the tracks. The dunes were peaceful in deep twilight, a last glow of light on their crests. We walked down the middle of the road holding hands, feeling a little high, a little sleepy. Around us were small rustlings in the grass, some mouse or insect settling down. Up on the foredune a light flickered in the window of Boris Margo's shack: someone had moved in after all.

At the bottom of the trail, where we should turn to climb up to Euphoria, we hesitated, and turned instead toward the beach. Between dunes, the beach opened before us, dusky pale sand edging the sea's cool mirror. These days there is so much light on the world, there is almost no nighttime to balance it. Just a pocket of darkness slipped in between the days. The whole sky lay floating on the skin of the water, its pinks and violets intermingled with blue, a gleam spreading along the horizon.

Bert skipped a stone. The gulls had all gone off to roost on the western side of a dune. The terns had left their nests for the night to float offshore, leaving the owl to take what he would. A sliver of moon came forward, materializing in the sky where it had hung since afternoon. Slowly lights offshore appeared, then stars. The Big Dipper reclined out over the water at Race Point, while other stars began to show themselves singly. Behind us, Antares hung down in the southeast, a bright star, christened "not Mars"—red like the planet, but not so belligerent.

THIRTEEN

The Thicket

It's summer now: I wonder if anything here knows. All of spring's spendthrift energy and carnal excitement has settled down into a purposeful mode; the songbirds are full of secrets, diving in and out among the green leaves. I see a flash of wing, the flick of a tail feather, and they're gone. Tall grasses, heavy with seed plumes, sway on the crest of the hill and rose hips fatten under the full petals. All day the southwest wind pushes at the walls, carrying a scent of hot, dry sand across the dunes. I hear a whistle, a trill of notes past the window. I step outside, and in a flurry of wings, something disappears into the brush.

Mornings, alone in the shack, I work well now. Bert is gone soon after daybreak, to crouch at the edge of the cranberry bog, chided by chickadees who interrupt their own business to investigate his doings. *Feebee*, they cry at first, inquiring, or a more companionable *tseet*, as they get used to him. Slowly the sculpture is taking shape as he goes on coiling loop over loop, fleshing out the framework of sticks with spirals of reed, making a figure in the air you can see into and through. The birds watch him curiously, and when he is gone, they fly in and out of his designs.

As for me, nobody can see what I'm doing. My hand moves over the paper, left to right; the pages close up; it's a secret.

My writing table sits under the back window, looking straight out onto a collapsing dune overgrown with bayberry, roses, and poison ivy. This thicket is deep and green and full of life, supporting rabbits, redwings, catbirds, finches, toads and ants. A network of roots props up the hill, and the ivy weaves a thick mat over the surface: there's no way in if you're human size. Mice sprint along invisible trails beneath the green canopy, but underneath the leaves the earth is sand.

I start off by pacing back and forth across all six feet of floor space, opening all the windows, chewing on my pen, and staring out as the world goes on beyond me. The shack is a retreat in the center of endless space, offering just the finest separation between inside and outside, its open windows and the cracks between its boards entangling me in a continuum of light and sound. *Okalee*——that's a redwing, sounding happy, but who knows? A goldfinch darts across the hill in a dazzle of yellow, crying *sweeeet*, and dives into the undergrowth. Almost immediately, an invisible force drags me onto the bottom bunk, where I lie motionless, staring upward at the mesh of wires that holds up the top mattress. These wires knot and regroup in a complex, dizzying pattern whose meaning I haven't been able to decipher. Someday I will crack the code. Finally, after twenty minutes' study I am able to get up and approach the table, sit down, and pull out a folder from the plastic file box. I have been working on a dozen new poems, with about twenty versions of each so far, the lines all crossed out and written over. There is an archaeological quality to the levels of revision here, descending strata of evolution approaching a first cause. I read the pages over, pretending someone else, someone very wise and very famous, has written them and I have only to transcribe her message. Finally I pull out the third poem in the pile, the piece of paper which still has the most white space on it, and begin.

I read the page over twice, making mental substitutions between the typed version and my scrawled emendations, then roll a sheet of paper into the typewriter, bang out the title, skip down five more spaces and retype the first line. Seven words, mostly good ones. Then the invisible force compels me to get up and turn on the radio. WOMR has the fishing report this morning and I listen thoughtfully to predictions of bluefish past Chatham Bars, bass running, "schoolies," out at Herring Cove, and somebody in Falmouth who's spotted a killer whale. I'm sure I can use this somewhere, and I conscientiously record the information in my journal, feeling virtuous and field-worthy. The naturalist at work, always alert to hints and signs. While I'm writing this down the reception starts to get fuzzy so I fiddle a bit with the antenna, aiming it toward Boston, then Truro, but it's no use, the batteries are low. I consider breaking out a new pack of Duracells, but switch it off instead and sit back down. I cross out the title and rewrite it, add a second line to the first, stare at it a while, and get up to make a cup of tea. This takes some time because I've filled the kettle up with a half gallon of cold pump water, and the little flame from the gas range puffs and sputters under its massive stainless steel load. It's no use sitting down until it boils, I tell myself. I'd no sooner get started then I'd have to get up again and lose my entire train of thought. While that train sits derailed somewhere in Iowa, I decide to make a great pot of tea in order to justify the effort expended. While the kettle heats, I strip the tags from a half dozen tea bags and lay out my fortunes in a row. "The noblest revenge is forgiveness." "Stay awake to make your dreams come true." And (my favorite today): "A gem is not polished without rubbing."

I ask myself: is this stuff lame or what? Do they PAY someone to make up these things? I think it must be ridiculously easy, and then I think: is this guy a WRITER? How much does he make, is he paid by the hour or by the fortune and could I get his job? What fortunes I would write, secure in the anonymity of the Salada Tea Company, each message folded inside a little paper pouch, softly scented with oolong and orange pekoe, dried leaves from the Orient. I could bring real intrigue to the art. Imagine the customer's face after dinner, his destiny in my hands, reading real omens, not advice: "Beware a dark woman with a shady past." "There is a killer in the room beside you."

The tea looks like swamp water. The overload of iron from the pump yields a greyish, streaky brew, like liquid aluminum. I add sugar and stand gazing out the window. Waves turn over down on the beach, and a cricket begins cheerfully scraping his wings in the high grass. What language is that? A herring gull lets loose his gargly cry, flying over, followed by a long *huoh, huoh, huoh*. I sit back down and stare at the page. Scratched over, rewritten, crossed out, the writing looks abstract, the words strange and foreign. I'm following something I can't see clearly, led on by hints and whispers, alert to every movement up ahead, where small lives hide themselves among the leaves. Teased forward, I lean toward a cry, a voice, three notes of song, ready to leave my body and fly after.

Where did the goldfinch go when he sliced through that wall of green and disappeared? I heard him ratchet in the leaves, and then no sign. The brush has grown thick and ivy trails across the path, closing up before me.

I return to what I've written, insert another word in the margin, trying to find my way through the maze. There is sense here, order beneath the confusion. Here. No. Not yet. Calm down, go slow, take it line by line, or word by word if need be. As my teabag says: "A gem is not polished without rubbing."

And rub I do. I write for a good hour—a patient, craftsmanlike hour, during which I forget for whole moments that at my age Eliot was already putting the finishing touches on *The Waste Land*, and just do the work. Version twenty-one seems less intimidating than version twenty; it's simpler, more willing to say something, even if it gets it wrong. Now it resembles an actual draft of a poem rather than a botched translation of the Dead Sea scrolls. It's a good morning's work, an hour of struggle and accomplishment, marking countless small victories over sloth, disorder, and self-doubt.

When I raise my head I'm astonished to find the world is still here. Sunlight lies in stripes across the tabletop, the pattern moving slowly at an angle, and a spider the size of a semicolon crawls over the screen.

Beyond the window, time speeds up in a flurry of bird song and a clash of wings. Flies swarm against the south wall where the full sun makes a tropics on the boards. A fleet of tree swallows is bombarding the side of the shack, picking the sleepy, sun-dazzled flies right out of the air. They dive and swoop at the wall, brushing past each other with eager wings and open mouths. Between the thumps and twitters of the feeding swallows, a catbird is practicing a new melody in the thicket. Three short notes and a trill, followed by a series of chirps and whistles. He pops his head up from the underbrush, tries a few measures, discards them and starts over. It seemed a good beginning to me, but he's dissatisfied. Such are the exigencies of art, teased along, coaxed into being, forever unsatisfactory. He gives one cry, breaks off, and disappears. I hear him rustle the leaves, and then nothing, though I sit very still and listen. If he calls again, I will go after him.

July

Nature is always the artist's best source of inspiration, but in its spiritual, not physical sense. In nature every object exists in relationship to other things. This is what we must seek.

—HANS HOFMANN,
The Hofmann School of Art, Provincetown

FOURTEEN

❧

Beach Days

In the afternoon, after lunch and a long rest in the cool shade of the shack, working or writing letters, when we've put down our books and the noon glare relents, in the afternoon, say two or even three o'clock, we go to the beach. We may walk along the shore in the mornings, picking up beach wrack, maybe playing at the edge of the waves, but then we remain in command of ourselves, in motion, and with some active connection to intelligence. Afternoons we just lie down. We spread towels the length of our bodies and stretch ourselves along them, flat to the ground, stunned under skylights, as we surrender flesh, blood, and brain cells to the wash and roar, the malleable sand and changing sky, the glaze of water breaking and skimming across the flat sand.

The sky is hazy; the old bedspread molds under my weight, shaping the sand in woman-shaped hills and valleys, making a negative print. I lie with my belly on the sand and surrender to physical bliss. First the long muscles let go; the body falls into the earth in parts and by increments: a shoulder releases, a hip, and the pelvic girdle unlocks, spilling soft, trusting organs downward. Intestines unknot to lie against the earth; I feel the pleasure of my spleen and liver as the sun warms through to deepest organs, a deep sigh in my diaphragm releasing. Emotions flow through my relaxed muscles and humming nerves.

The sun, just crossed over from Asia, is doing its own Turkish massage, heating the small of my back, probing between my shoulder blades to unroot a knotted tendon, melting the little bones of my neck like syrup. My legs lengthen as the hip joints unlock. My face goes calm and slack and I gaze like a serpent, dimly aware, a single gaze of this and then this, threaded through slitted eyes.

Looking, staring, because there is nothing to see, because you can only see a single thing, and then another. A sanderling chases the water's edge in a state of continuous panic, cloud shadows float across the sand, and something dark out there caught in the second tier of waves turns over and over, thrown to shore and hauled back: a log, a rubber tube, a dead shark. A dune tour bumps down the beach, swaying in the deep ruts of other jeep tracks, and passes slowly; I raise one arm to wave to them. Our first summer here we snubbed the tourists, but we're over that now. When I turn over, millions of grains of sand stick to my thighs, covering me with a new carapace, a skin of sand, ivory and brown with black flecks and orange ones and grey, all glistening with oil.

Looking, listening, unguarded, I float in that aptly named "oceanic state," in which prayer, meditation, and genius are one. "Genius," declared the inventor Edwin Land, "is nothing more than a momentary cessation of stupidity." Thoughts and feelings previously unrelated have time to interact and group themselves into new formations. This state requires an ability to submit, a feeling of safety in which the mind is free to detach a little from immediate concerns, best accomplished where there are no lions about. Most of all it requires time. Two ends curving around to meet one another, the beginning meeting the end. Giving up control, I submit to the sun, its slow hours marking a passage across the prehistoric sky.

Bert stretches and hauls himself from the sand to saunter down to the water; I close my eyes and sink deeper. I might lie here forever in this relaxed, druggy state, sweating under blue clouds, the sea birds fluttering and swooping overhead. The pound of the surf surges through me; I slide my hands under the sand, wallow, make hollows for my knees and elbows, heap up a pillow for my head, swimming in a bliss as mild as bread dough. I'm slung out like a slab of fish, delirious, serene, stippled and sun-anointed. Look at the cool cool water lathering up the beach, waves turning and shaping, scrubbing the world up into a glare and shine.

I lie here forever at peace until a frozen walrus comes blowing up from behind, puffing and tossing sparks of icy water into the air. They hit my back like fat on a griddle and I turn to snarl at my beloved in wifely walrus-fashion.

Bert stands exultant above me, buffing his chest with a towel, shouting. "You've got to get in! It's great!" He shouts this though I am lying right at his feet, directly, as it happens, in the wake of his spray, and drops beside me, joyous, panting with pride. "You need to get your head in. Everything is gone, the cold takes it all away, you feel great." I tell him I feel just lovely already thank you and could he please move his frigid flesh a little to the right, if he would be ever so kind. He shakes his head in disbelief, spraying drops of glacial water in all directions.

Then he's all over me, rubbing and bouncing with glee. "You are so sleek and soft and warm!" he declares, burrowing his head into my armpit, rubbing my naked back with his cold, wet, salty, seaweedy hand.

"And you smell like Charlie the Tuna."

"Dolphin. I'm a mammal, you know. And you better watch out: sometimes they get very sexual with their trainers." He rolls over on his back then, puffing out air, delighted with himself.

It's July, but the water is still cold. The water on this shore will always be cold. I lie on the beach until my bones are hot and I can feel my eyeballs burn. I expect to cause a small explosion when I touch the waves, water hissing like lava, steam flying up around me. I hang back at the edge, letting myself in slowly, an inch at a time, cringing with an exquisite torture Bert can never comprehend. "You've gotta get right in!" he yells in an encouraging tone, as I measure millimeters of increment from hip to belly to breast, shuddering and turning back as a wave laps my shoulders. I don't "gotta" do anything.

It is genius to nobly do nothing when to do anything more would be stupid. Try on a winter day to picture this scene, that the world is so forgiving you can lie almost naked with your eyes closed beside the brimming ocean. On a clear day, when the sun is low enough not to burn your eyes, look out to the horizon and feel how the earth curves out in a broad sweep away from you. Waves along the sand bar are breaking low—just folding over, the only flourish on the quiet water this afternoon. Scrunching up sand in handfuls, in fistfuls, let the golden grains of sand flow warm between your fingers—tiny fragments of world, come to this.

These beach days are brief. True summer on the back shore doesn't begin until July and lasts eight weeks, nine if we're lucky, from July Fourth to the soft close of Labor Day, when the September waters begin to cool and the sunlight stretches long and thin. For all the endless feeling of these days, they are few, though rich and wide inside. We feel a loosening and freedom of the body, a safety in the warmth of the earth against us, under blue skies. All summer under the great fire we worship memories of summer, of slow, languid water, sleepy afternoons, the drowsy wash of tides in the brain.

A wave falls forward and the water spreads itself flat, gently wavering with light, just a moment before the undertow returns and it is pulled back, sucked down to the cold depths. Everything stops a moment; there's a tug, a hesitation. The sky is still; some high, thin clouds are moving out to the north, white whippy cirrus, mostly ice crystals. A slick of water glazes the shore where broken waves flow out across the flats, percolating down through the brown sand. Out past the sandbar a white boat is riding, rising and falling from sight, and a whale blows a spout of foam up to the sky. There's a noise of engines offshore, a radio playing; and beyond us, at the edge of our vision, way up in the high, blue sky, there is nothing, and there it all ends.

Some afternoons we walk the two and a half miles to Race Point, and we "go to the beach" with the rest of the world. We arrive heavy-footed, without coolers, blankets, or radios, and join for a while in the summer festival, where children dig immense holes at the tide's edge and leave them to fill with water, and frisbees and paddleballs fly back and forth. Hunkered down on the hot sand, I lust after my neighbors' six-packs, their beer cans floated like wondrous icebergs in styrofoam chests, packages of chips that make an exaggerated crunch in the mouth, their wedges of cold, bright pink watermelon. Mick Jagger is singing, the whole London Bach Choir behind him, with an itchy, transistor urgency: *ya cahn't always get what ya wa-hant.* Thou shalt not covet thy neighbor's cooler. I take a long swig from my canteen and look away from temptation.

This beach is noisy, littered with plastic toys and sandwich wrappers, herringboned with jeep tracks, jumpy with radios and absolutely redolent of coconut oil. The surf sounds like the hiss of a thousand pop-tops being pulled back, a continual party. It's wonderful, a shot of pure adrenalin on those days when we visit as if dropped from the moon. The people are clean and pretty; they look delicate next to our tanned, salty skin and sun-washed shirts. Most have a flush of pink on their noses and shoulder blades, and the wide-awake air of visitors. It seems brighter here, hotter. I shade my eyes to follow a kite up into the sky—a yellow bird with an enormous tail and two shimmering threads holding it. A baby girl is making hand-drip castles, then sitting on them. In the waves a small boy paddles ecstatic, clutching a small surfboard. Two mothers trail their feet back and forth in the water, looking off to the horizon, scanning for children, speaking easily without looking at one another. Bert is scavenging at the high tide line, bending and dipping like a long-legged bird, a heron or crane, peering with scholarly precision at the sand. His hands are full of sticks and he has stuck bits of bright nylon rope into his baseball cap and generally he appears festooned and serious.

This going to the beach is something new under the sun. We have had to learn pleasure here. For centuries the beach was a place to walk and forage, to search the horizon for ships or weather, cast for fish or launch boats. It was a serious place, a work place. The water was for keeping out of; even the fishermen didn't know how to swim.

Swimmers in the thirties swam, or sank, fully clothed in woolen shirts and knee-length pants, stockings, caps and rubber shoes. They were lucky to stay afloat at all when their clothes waterlogged and tangled, growing heavy as armor. Now in ceremonial attire, nearly naked, hugging the earth and wallowing in sand, we worship pleasure. Our vestments are little bits of cloth, stretchy material, and our skin glistens with precious tropical oils. We squint under our sun hats and wear dark glasses against the light we never turn to see. Where else do you see people lie down right on the earth? We lie on this new shore in our skin, red and brown and smeared with unguents, undefended and secure, and give in like animals to the heat. And though the waves scrub up on the sand and the wind blows over our heads, it may be that the beach will never relinquish its new odor of coconut and palm kernels, as Massachusetts dreams, briefly, that she is Tahiti before the missionaries.

We leave before the beach starts to empty, walk back slowly and let the pretty carnival get small and quiet behind. It feels a little melancholy to leave the people behind, to hear the human sounds grow small. Behind us, they pack up their cars and drive away to rented rooms; they walk down streets full of voices, past restaurants and bars with music spilling from their open doors. It is melancholy, and I know why melancholy can be such a sweet emotion, a thoughtful sadness made mostly out of pleasure but with more shadings than pleasure, something sweet set against deep shadows. The only sadness is the thought, a gloom back-lit by the low sun. It grows quickly peaceful as we walk along, and around a bend or two we have lost the feeling of that world. The empty beach lies before us; the shack sits up in the distance, small against the hill, and there's a white line leading up to it, the little trail made by our own two sets of footprints, scuffed by us day by day as we go down to the beach and back.

FIFTEEN

❦

At Evening

Evenings drying dishes by lamplight, the radio giving intimate details of weather. We pick up odd stations here, signals driven to this outpost thrust into the sea. Beneath the west window over the stove, a towel flaps on its hook. It gusts and falls, leaps and returns in irregular beats. We lower the window with a rope on a pulley as evening begins. The stars come out just as the fishing boats are lighting their lamps—they glimmer in the distance the same pure white. Watching them, I picture myself on the deck of a sailing boat, listening to high laughter, drinking from a glass with ice. Here in the privacy and shadows of the shack, I conjure voices and lighted places. But I know I would look back and crave the familiar secrets of this place, try to imagine myself here again.

I move around the room, putting away dishes, washing the glass chimneys and leaving them to glint on the counter as they dry. Sound of a cup lifted from the shelf and set down, the teabag ripping open. The washbowl rattles in the sink's uneven bottom. Our routines here have become routine: hauling water, sweeping, washing dishes in a basin, setting them to dry in the old yellow rack: these echo with the resonance of habit and repetition. Brown shadows glide up the walls and a soft, rose glow lies along the dunes. The waves subside in a rush, sounding far away.

Crackle of paper being wadded into a ball, pages of a newspaper turning. Shapes are distinct, then not quite so: the tilted deck post, the clothesline, appear in stark outline; then their lines are reabsorbed. Sand hills go ivory, ecru, brown. Four separate white lights appear at the horizon, off to the east, fishing boats anchoring for the night.

Light the first lamp: a flame catches the wick. It is contained, to itself, a light so small and quick, upburning in space. Place the bowed chimney down though, and the light leaps into the glass, and flares and shines all around, throwing shelves and corners, tables and chairs, into new dimensions of depth and shadow. Just two or three small flames, each a wick dipped in oil, their light magnified, reflected, and sent out multiplied by blown glass. The red covers on the bunks glow like a king's velvet. Stainless steel forks and spoons twinkle in the rack and the old wood warms to a deeper brown, crusted with scars and stains, the marks of old use.

I sit at the table writing in my journal. The book is filling with summer scenes, incidents, ideas—it pleases me to keep writing, to balance whole sentences on a thought or an impression, each one set down here and assigned a place. It gets darker and I begin to see my face in the window, translucent, like looking through water. Eyes, the darkest, catching light, a sweep of hair fallen over my forehead. Behind my eyes, across my temples, above my cheekbones, the northern edge of the water draws a line at the sky. My nose floats on the still, navy-blue water; my forehead is superimposed on the blue-grey horizon. I reach out my hand toward the glass and in my palm, exactly in the middle of my palm, is the first white star.

We do not talk. Bert lies on the bed, turning the pages of a book, the radio tuned to a whisper at his ear, a dream of baseball. In a single room, in separate pools of light, with not six feet between us, we make a spaciousness of the mind. The wind is wuthering across the dunes—a grating undertone of sand dragged across sand. I can barely hear the water now. New moon tonight: it will be dark and there will be stars. I'm distracted by a *thunk-thunk* at the window, and I look up. A brown moth bats at the pane, confused by our lights. Something creaks and cricks and scratches in the wall under the east window, some insect in the wood, a sound just at the threshold of hearing.

My hand pushes a huge, soft shadow across the page as I write. *Look up.* Now the window is blank and my face is a portrait lighted from one side. Nothing looks through me now—all that world is held behind my eyes, invisible, opening out behind. Another life, a deeper one, is there. On this side I cannot see it, except for that brief glimpse at dusk, in the momentary translucence of flesh and sky. How quickly it closes, uncertainly remembered. The flame jerks and straightens and my hand's shadow flows over the page as I sit quietly writing at the end of the day.

SIXTEEN

Sanctuary

It is almost noon, warm and muggy, and the fog that has drifted in and out of the valleys all morning is breaking up and starting to blow across the sand in thin transparent ribbons. I've wandered back behind the second line of dunes, through marshes and scrub woods, led on by a quail whose cheerful whistle continually receded before me. Other sounds come from far off: a jeep takes the hill with a snarl and a clash of gears, and in the distance a crow protests some real or perceived invasion. Sight flies to the limits of the visible; the world closes in, bounded by haze. A bird dives into a patch of green and disappears.

On a grey day, the dunes are uninhabited. Even the old sun is absent, blanked out in a white sky. Sand dunes the color of clouds rise up in huge drifts, one beyond another, and flow away. The sand has a clean texture, swept by long, even winds. Small birds and insects scratch their marks across the surface. A vole swam up a bank ahead of me as I climbed, scrambling wildly as sand streamed past his claws; eyes closed, he willed not to see me. I passed a little downy woodpecker clinging to a stunted oak. Rabbit pellets marked the entrance to a bayberry thicket and there were deer tracks right out in the open, though the deer, as usual, were nowhere to be seen.

I know the deer walk here every day. Wholly ordinary, calm and free, they walk in their own lives as if there were only one world, as if history had never happened. In the hour before dawn, or at twilight, they might step fully into the open. Their wide ears quiver, their heads swing round, their soft black lips part inquiringly. By day they lie hidden in deep brush; they see us coming and quietly withdraw into the trees.

There is no path here; the country lies open, hot and still. In troughs between the dunes, sheltered from wind and salt spray, the sand grows stunted woods of pitch pine and scrub oak. Grey-green poverty grass sits up in tufts of its own root hairs, brandishing little yellow flowers, and the ground is crusted with ant hills, moss, pine needles decaying into earth. Lichens spring up underfoot: reindeer moss and old man's beard, tiny elaborate structures that live a hundred years, making soil out of bare rock. The ones called British soldiers prick up their scarlet points.

These woods are poor, bent and twisted inward as if they would consume themselves. To enter them I have to stoop and duck my head, checked by branches at shoulder height. Woody fingers scratch at my face. A horsefly fumbles past, listing like an awkward spaceship, and disappears into the fissures of a dead tree. Then a blue jay hollers out his name like an insult: *jaaaaay*, and flaps off. And never the deer, in all my time here, never the deer, only their tracks that lead straight up the side of a hill, and step off into midair.

As I press ahead, the woods close up. I push into the tall trees and a red squirrel scolds *get-get-get*, stomps twice with all four feet, twirls his tail furiously, and flees into the undergrowth. I hear the woods calling to itself, crying warnings and diving under cover, and where I stand the branches have gone still.

The only thing for it is to stop and let the woods find me. I sit down with my back against the trunk of a pine, my feet in pine needles, the sun on my legs, and wait while the disturbance dies down. The woods come to me first as a smell of warm stone, dust, and the resinous odors of pine, fragrant and slightly bitter. I sit and examine the nearest tree, this one's brother, with close attention. Its heavy bark is coated with a yellow fungus; breathing out oxygen, it twists upward to let the sun touch it. A gold light falls on the pine needles. A box turtle steps slowly, deliberately across the sand; I see its glittering red eye, its unhurried step, treading across a complete world. A woodpecker hangs upside down on a branch about eight feet up—he makes the tree sway back and forth as he drums it, raining down wood chips. He's a headbanger, convulsive, his whole body contorted with hammering. Rat-a-tat. In the distance, a small plane dips low against the hill, circling in for a landing at Race Point.

If you look carefully at a patch of ground, a square yard or so, look long and carefully, you don't soon run out of looking. Little brown ants, grains of sand, twigs and seeds and pine needles. Bits of curling bark. All along the ground, roots and stems and runners tether each plant to the thin earth, each live thing reaching into space, floating itself on the air. Under the dry pine needles are wet, blackening ones, a little grainy soil under that, then sand again. A harvestman spider crawls over my shoe, lifting delicate, modular legs singly, light as a creature on the moon, holding on with sticky footpads lest a breath blow him away. That cigarette filter may lie there for two thousand years. Fecklessly dropped, it blew into this shade, finding refuge at the base of a pine. It is white, cylindrical, neat and oddly unobjectionable, taking up its small allotment of space without presuming. What is that bird? A sweet chirrup keeps darting in and out of hearing. Teasing, clear, it seems to come from first one side, then the other.

It was so quiet I could hear the leaves breathe. I heard the sea sucking far below, faint and constant, half a mile off; the sound came through the trees, a great current flowing across the land and into my body, its waves breaking up against whorls of brain matter. My blood lunged and raced down black tunnels of arteries, thrust from the heart's sealed chambers.

The tree at my back felt rough, marking my skin with the pattern of its bark. The trees live longer than we do, living more slowly. Light entered the slits of my eyes and I could feel the tree breathe behind me, riding the world around, gripping the earth, splitting upward.

If another presence came into my mind—a call, a touch—I might become the forest to be entered. Light flashed on every branch, but inside me it was dark. Shadows moved along the ground, leaves turned, and the little hairs on my arm stood up.

A thin boundary, finer than a bubble, thinner than a cell wall, stretched and pulled between inside and out, self and world. If this boundary is washed away I will disappear—that thought occurred and went under, like a bottle in a wave raised up and pulled down again. Rained on my head, the weight of sunlight, particles of odor, infinitesimal atoms of pine and salt and dust. The air leaned heavily against my skin, and then only a thin edge of me was left, a surface tension, an old loyalty of molecules to a remembered order. I could have let it go and never stood up again, it was that close. Then a shape flew past—so quickly, with such force—like something shot from the trees, a missile, a self-guided arrow, a blackbird calling.

Was it the bird's call that pulled me back? Two notes, bright and sharp—at the last minute I asked myself: "What bird is that?" and hauled myself back into awareness.

If I had stood up then my legs would have wobbled and shook. The woods were closed again, leaving no place to remind me where I was woven in so delicately, momentarily. Light slanted between the trees, glinted on a stick not quite dry, and pebbles and particles and stone-colored lichens all sat clear in their own right. From oak to pine, across the plum thicket and roses, a blackbird flew straight across the sky, crying.

When I stood up at last I found a large red tick clinging to the cuff of my sock, holding on with a vast and stupid hunger. Its grip was so tight and passionate that I could not detach it. Sensing blood, body heat, it clutched its flat, round body to the weave of a sock, burrowed down as far as need would carry it toward the re- union of flesh; if it had to eat through a world of sock meat it would, to cross that frontier, full of yearning.

I flicked it with my finger, then knocked at it with a stick, and scraped the side of the stick across the threads, but it wouldn't budge. "That's a sock, dummy!" I explained. It only knew how to hold on; it could not reconsider. This smallest speck, this univer- sal parasite wanted to be my brother, to share with me every germ of its former lives. Eight legs, eight filaments adhered, held on with blood lust. Drink me slowly, small and powerful, full of dis- ease, stupefied with blind desire. Drink me up, oh Rocky Moun- tain Fever, Lyme Disease, Plague, Typhus: the blood-sucker's of- ferings. Resigned, then, to its friendship, I took off my sock, rolled it in my hand, and set off walking stiffly toward the marshy meadow behind the shack. Everywhere I stepped, ants were marching with me, small specific lives, faintest perceptions of order: this earth is so strange, what do we ever know? A dun- colored butterfly came to light on my shoulder but changed her aim at the last second. The sun came out in a hazy sky, and it began to turn hot. Midges swarmed and quivered, banging into my forehead, swimming in my breath. I walked from shade to light, out of light into shadow, uphill and down, and up again.

In the distance the line of sand was pink, the roofline of Eu- phoria etched on the hill beyond. A pleasant, rank odor hung over the marsh, and flies bumped slowly against the grassheads. As I came over the rise, there below me, four deer were feeding. One looked up and turned her head to look at me, taking me in with wide wet eyes. Nostrils flared forward, large round eyes on the sides of her head, eyes of the hunted. She gazed long, with mild and tranquil interest, took a single step away, then stopped and turned back again to her grazing.

SEVENTEEN

✺

Dog Days

Footprints circle the shack, not ours. Mouse, rabbit, toad, the prints read. We lay sleeping; we knew nothing. Maybe a change in the wind made us turn over, the scratch of sand tossed up against the shingles. Warm shapes moved near us in the dark; they crept along the roof and under the floor, and slipped away on padded paws. Past midnight a skunk nosed the garbage pail, fearless, trailing must, his thick, swampy odor caught in our throats. We coughed, turned over, dreaming skunk.

It's hot, the sun is high up in the sky, already baking the dunes. We woke late this morning, heavy and stale after a night of sticky heat. Bert grumbles through breakfast: it requires three matches, a sound curse, and the banging of a pot lid to light the stove. The chair in its usual place offends him, the bread is stale, there is no milk for tea. I try not to take it personally: Bert's moods are like the weather, dramatic but fleeting. "Emoting," he calls it. He sits down and stares out the window, with faraway, unseeing eyes.

"What are you thinking?" I ask.

He grins over at me. "Nothing much. Murder, arson, ruin . . . The usual."

"Oh good," I tell him, letting out a breath. "I thought it was me."

We're living under the Dog Star. Sirius, lodged in the nose of Canis Major, is closest to the sun now, bringing heat and pestilence. The brightest fixed star in the sky, he lights our discontent. These dog days find us simmering in heat; flies whine at the screens, and at evening the eerie buzz of mosquitoes haunts the air as they levitate on currents, finding their way to us over miles of grass and dunes. In the black night, in our beds, we're prisoners to a single thought, a whine at our ears drilling sleep as one mosquito grazes the dark.

A pair of tree swallows is flying back and forth from their nest, feeding their insatiable chicks. They make little murmuring noises as they pass over the deck, seemingly bothered by my presence. These days they work frantically from dawn to night to satisfy ungrateful hungers. A head fills the round hole of the bird box; as a parent nears, the head becomes all mouth opening, turned inside out. How they cry, these giant hungry babies. The chicks are almost big enough to leave the nest, but these days nothing moves. Everything stalls, waits, delays completion. Down on the beach a pair of terns is guarding a clutch of eggs that will not hatch. All the other nests have chicks, but this nest sits and spoils; the parents wait, unable to count time.

A white sheen rises over the water; the sun hangs low, broadcasting shimmering heat rays across the surface. The beach is heaped with seaweed: fucus, codium, sargassum, kelp, sea lettuce, all rotting in the heat. There's a rank smell and no wind. Sandfleas rise up murmuring in the dead weeds, and as the day wears on the greenheads appear, vicious and single-minded, honing in on all defenseless flesh.

Last week the Park Service closed the beach from Race Point to High Head—the tern and plover chicks have hatched—and the fishermen are mad. They announced a protest for yesterday: some of the RV clubs planned to meet at Race Point Beach and line up their vehicles along the border of the prohibited area. A show of force: I wonder if the plovers were intimidated. Ill will simmers everywhere. Now the terns begin screaming down on the beach; then the swallows return and fly at me, crying and circling over my head—as if I had anything to do with their troubles.

My discomfort grows. My hair lies limp against my neck. A kiss is damp and sticky. The refrigerator has quit working three times since yesterday. By the time we get it running again the meat has started to spoil.

Why do the animals hide, why do bugs bite, why do I have a body that sweats and bleeds and itches and lies about sighing? Insects," according to Saint Augustine, "remind us of the inconvenience of the mortal state." Is it my fault for wanting the world to be what I want it to be? I can't seem to accept that this place doesn't need me, that I'm neither welcome nor unwelcome. And also, I think too much.

"Do you think there's something wrong with me?" I finally ask Bert, trying to sound casual.

"Excuse me?"

"Something fundamentally wrong, deep down, that makes it impossible for me to fit in, to adjust to things."

"Oh yeah," he says, looking thoughtful. "Yeah. You're a nut."

As summer wears on, I'm more and more aware of my inability to be a part of this landscape which I love. I feel caught between two worlds, standing on the border of one, gazing longingly into the other. My curiosity betrays me, spying on the birds and animals.

Just watch and here he comes, hopping out from under a rose bush into a clear circle of sand, this most anxious heir of all creation. The rabbit sits back on his big feet, chewing the grass tips one after another, bending down the stalks, tasting only the tenderest parts and moving on. Gangly, young, unevenly put together, his ears hang askew, pointing extravagantly in opposite directions. Big ears, big feet, he's all attachments to a compact little body. On his own this morning, he's a baby gourmet, weighing the succulence of grass tip and blade, seed head and blossom, giddy with choice. Even so, he won't forget himself entirely. The rabbit's eye is bright and unmoving. He looks straight ahead, in profile like an Egyptian relief, trying to catch sounds with the hot, sensitive skin of his ears, ready to run at any movement, but not wanting to, wanting only to stay and graze upon this intoxicating bounty of summer green. He is all youth in his dilemma, his fresh hunger and candid look around at every danger. Rabbit-like, exactly. New actor in an old role, how well he plays "rabbit," how he masters himself in it already.

Now he sees me, and seems to freeze and make himself small without moving. He waits, performing whatever passes for deciding in his morsel of a brain, then nibbles, stops, then takes another bite.

Yesterday, while moving some old boards, I uncovered a colony of ants under a stack of two-by-fours behind the shack. They went into a great commotion getting out from under my shadow. The dowager queen, shiny as black glass, was hurriedly shoved down a hole by her military escort. Nurse ants nudged eggs and larvae ahead of them; little flesh-pink pods tumbled over one another as the workers scrambled back and forth dismantling top secret installations. I stared a while at the unroofed architecture of highways and cathedrals and watched the city go up in a panic.

Ants we see everywhere, more ants than rabbits. Ants are in the sand and in the rock: minute, willful beings burrowing under fence posts and kitchen counters. They trail across the path, swarm over flat stones, crawl along flowers and up weed stalks, erupting out of bare dirt. Ant hills, ant columns, solitary ants scurrying back to the nest, bearing their remarkable burdens, and never minding the world. They eat grease and sugar, blossoms, dead beetles, and motor oil alike. What the planet gives they take, what they encounter they do not question, and whatever happens with the rest of creation remains a matter of the dimmest interest. Their fate hangs on the disposition of ant, on one particular community of saints, all females, abiding here in the desert.

Were they aware of me looking at them? In spite of all the ruckus, I don't think so. It's more likely the upheaval was caused by the sudden light, or change of air temperature, than by any awareness of my presence. Most of the time they go on, underfoot and around us, talking their private talk, mumbling invocations, acknowledging no other world. The rabbit knows more of me, though this makes him wary, and as a result, I probably know him less.

The rabbit hops off down the hill, going about his business, and I wonder, for the hundredth time this week, what mine is here. It is possible to live here every day, for weeks and into months, and see, essentially, nothing. You can study signs, tracks, clues, and still never be able to say what you've missed. You can live in the world, even in a place as bare and bright and close to the bone as this one, and never see the world. There are white-tailed deer in the marshes, foxes glimpsed by the side of the trail, who disappear, nose first, into the bushes. Beach mice scurry under grass cover, in direct relation with grass and with the marsh hawk circling above: invisible vectors connect them, force lines of desire and shared DNA. They squeeze through holes in the boards on summer nights to steal our crumbs and chew up bits of cotton scarves or socks for nests, yet our relation is casual, based on accidents of proximity and economics: we have goods between us, not substance, as in the equation of grass, mouse, harrier. To be a mouse is to fear the shadow of the hawk and to thrive on the new grass, to grow tender and fat to feed the winged shadow made of mouse and grass. We inhabit this common ground with varying degrees of curiosity or unease. The mouse is a spoiler and a quiet thief, stealing tastes of bread and cotton in unwitting intimacy by night. To the hawk, I'm a minor annoyance, set in the middle of her flight path, while every tern detests the very shape of my shadow. The ant discounts me completely, due to her utter lack of imagination; the rabbit eats, watches, and bewares. The comb-foot spider who hangs her frowzy web from the porch rail, secured to the underside of the third step of the shack Euphoria, conveniently near the reeking trash can, does not know where she is, or care particularly. And though I walk across her wooden firmament every morning and make her whole universe shake, in that universe I do not, in fact, exist.

EIGHTEEN

❧

Talking in the Dark

All night the flame whiffs and whooshes under the hood of the little propane refrigerator, its motor struggling in the heat to make cold. In the dark the pilot light glows yellow. Striking a match, I turn the stove dial, and gas rushes toward the flame. Bert wakes to ask sleepily if I'm all right, do I need him. Blue flame leaps in cabin darkness, a floorboard creaks, a teacup scratches across the table top. Impossible to move silently.

It is some unnamed, unchristian hour past midnight. I'm sick with fever, chills, and a deep, dull pain in my gut. For hours I've been heating endless kettles, drinking tea and refilling the hot water bottle, trying to send warmth into the cold empty spaces between my cells. Some hours ago I routed Bert out of the lower bunk and sent him up top to sleep. Now, bed to window, window to door, and back again, I mark the hours until morning.

The dark in the room is a physical presence, filling every corner, heavy as water. Space begins at my face, and presses back at my outstretched hand; outside, the planet turns, stars hiss and flare, and small animals snuff beneath the grasses. I walk to the door and lean against the screen: dark as it is on this hill, over the water is darkest night. Fog-shrouded, two or three miles out, some boats are riding at anchor, the lights on their masts flickering through the vapor. Highland Light sweeps a faint beam against the hill, then turns away. Sweat glazes my face and shoulders and a shiver slides up my legs.

I lean there, moony in the dark. The screen feels soft and grainy, its mesh stretching under my hand. The little hook and eye digs into my arm and I move aside slightly. A very small contraption—a bent hook, no bigger than a nail, and a little hole to pass it through. Warm air flows freely through the wires. Frenchie said the dead take walks together on these moonless nights, strolling with lighted candles across the crests of the dunes. Why do they need candles if they are dead, I asked. She frowned at that. I don't need ghosts to scare me. My worst dreams are the simplest, inner visions I have no defense against here in the dark.

Yesterday, while Bert was out working in the dunes, a man came to the door carrying a long stick and a gallon of Gallo red. He leaned on the screen and looked in at me: "Hi." I looked up and he was there; I had not heard him coming. I was lying on the bed in a t-shirt and shorts, my papers spread all around. I could see this little hook and eye fastening the screen—so flimsy I could rip it with my hands. His smile stayed too long; he stood with the light behind him, between me and the outside, my back against the wall.

He was drunk, and, as it turned out, meant no harm. I didn't know that. I asked what he wanted and got up to walk to the door, assuming an authority I could never back up. He let me pass. It was better outside somehow, not to feel trapped. He sat on the step and drank from the bottle. Nothing happened. He left after a while, after his being there had almost begun to seem normal, more an annoyance than a terror, though I knew it could turn in an instant. He got bored and staggered down to the beach, leaving the empty jug on the step. I could see him weaving in and out of sight below, walking up and down, drunk, and crazy from too much sun, shaking his stick at the hills like some Moses.

Now I stand at the door, staring into the dark while my mind chews up old worries, endless chatter. How long until morning?

First the dark will thin a little, and shadows will rise up from the black ground. Then pink streaks will appear in the sky. From the corner of the east window, between two angles of wood and glass, the sun will rise up out of the water. Gulls will cry out rudely. I throw the blanket from my shoulders as a sweat sheen washes my skin; the muscles of my neck and shoulders tighten. Dark fills up the world.

Tonight I wish for a fluorescent-lit motel: gleaming white porcelain, hot and cold water flowing at a touch, switching channels on the buzzing cable. Late-night TV, a refuge in the nowhere world of sickness and insomnia, to take me out of myself.

Instead I am thoroughly here, feeling my body flush and chill, the greasy feel of my skin, the thick blood pushing through my veins, feeling the several deaths that live in my body wriggle up like spiders, smelling it. That burning when you pee means infection in the urinary tract. Infections like this start quickly, race up the body through filaments, every system connected. Before sulfa, penicillin, how many died of a strange germ at the orifice, a blocked duct, fever and chills?

The fever enlarges me; vague, swollen, my skin heats the air. Who can say where I end and the night begins? I'm hot, burning, a languid coal; the pain in my abdomen and lower back is deep, a root going into the ground, a stake driven through the flesh, down through mattress, chair, floorboards, and into the center of the earth. I'm grateful at least for the foresight that goaded me to hoard Bactrim, after a horrible night two years ago when I woke up sicker than this, and had to hike into town in a rainstorm the next morning. Waiting in the doctor's office, wringing wet, sick and sleepless and sour smelling, the fever spiking up, I felt like a refugee presenting myself at a mission hospital. Then to trudge to the pharmacy and back out again. Laid me up for a week. After that I managed to convince my doctor I could be trusted with a single course of sulfa.

With sulfa you drink lots of water or burn up inside. Drink water and piss in the dark. This is what it comes to, on a dark, close night, squatting over a decommissioned lobster pot beside the door, squeezing out dark, spare drops of burning urine. Any illusions I may have cherished about myself disappear from this pose. I look out into the sky and see nothing, and feel myself a voyager in space, this earth a satellite, a spaceship carrying me out of time. It makes me think of Laika, that sad little dog the Russians sent up, who circled the earth and died, poison in her food when the oxygen ran out.

Sick, sick in the night, sick body, sick spirit, sick heart. I think sick thoughts; I sing my sick lament. Hot forehead, cold feet, marble feet, cold wet stink of the body corpse. Herb tea and the hair rising on my arms, dread as before lightning: something gonna get me. All this to repel a single invasion, to keep the strange cells from joining my body. Fear the flea on the hair of a mouse, bacteria on a fly's foot, the sucking kiss of a deer tick, pestilence; fear the stranger in the body. Something foreign enters, undermines, and you shrivel like an apple on the stem, gnarls and canker, wormy at the heart. How does death get in, that invisible worm? Where did the fatal germ come from?

Fear the stranger. The man leaning against the screen, holding the door shut with his body, his lounging pose of ease, his sunburned face, his wine-blurred, self-loving smile. He crept up so quietly. How long had he been standing there when I looked up? And before? Walking around the shack, looking, touching. Wondering at first was there anyone here, peering in to find it was only one woman.

I put the lid on the pot, furtive, like a cat kicking dirt over the spot, never find me out. I would like to lie down in a long white tub with hot water up to the rim, lie back in it, let everything float, marry my fever to the hot water, and wash it out. The clean, bleachy smell of towels fluffed in a hot air dryer, spun around and around until all the fibers separate, so fat and soft. Bright bright overhead light, and that green or slate-blue motel room carpet. Read the paper all the way through, business pages and obituaries of strangers, yard sales on the north shore, zoning meetings in Milton. Read of far away lives, other people's problems. See what they all died of, what they're fighting about. Funny I think of a motel, not a house. Is my idea of home, then, a room at the Holiday Inn, buzzing fluorescent fixtures, dead bolt, sample bottles of shampoo, bad art on the walls?

Sleep won't come; this night is endless. The peacefully snoring beast in the upper bunk lies eons away, no help to me, as far apart as one soul from another in Hades. Something bumps against the shack outside, some sniffing nocturnal animal, one of the track-makers I'll never see. You might make anything out of these night sounds, but they are usually only mice. I get up, put on more hot water, lie down on the bed and wait for morning.

NINETEEN

Tempest

All day it was so hot the world burned. The water slid back and
forth along shore, uncoiling like a muscle. Sand sizzled as the
waves broke and drew back, dragging pebbles into the cool depths
where they bounced and simmered in the froth.

Tern chicks crouch on hot sand under this breathless sun. They
hide in jeep tracks or in footprints for shade, while their parents
fly back and forth, making sharp cries and diving over the water.
The birds' voices are shrill, hysterical in the heat. Back and forth
they fly, searching, crying, then they stop against the air, fold their
wings and plunge straight down, twisting slightly with wings back
and head tucked for a deadfall dive, shearing off just at the surface. They rise and dive again and again for the small fish, flying
endlessly back and forth from their hot nests to the glaring surface
of the water. They are so pure a white, so definite and sleek and
gleaming a white and their cries are like the sound of wires
dragged across metal, high and cutting, yet distant as a signal
from space.

I stood chest-deep in the current, feeling the salt sting my insect-
bitten skin. I squinted up at the sky where blue and silver lights
bounced into my eyes. The sun had weight, leaning on my bare
shoulders, leaving a hot scar on the flesh it pressed. The pigment

in my cells rushed forward to darken, little dye pots breaking open and spilling to dim the gleam of pale skin. Drying myself, I brushed glowing crystals of quartz from my arms and legs, each grain separate and precise and final as my flesh is not: one atom of silicon nested between four atoms of oxygen in exquisite, repetitive symmetry. Time made these crystals: uncounted, undisturbed quantities of time, balancing molecule on molecule. Cell by cell, over millions of years, my body is preserved in stone: patterns of tissue and muscle fiber replaced as semiprecious stones, the spirit light of bone growing ever more stable. Agate, jasper, amethyst, lapis . . . a sea change, pearls that were my eyes, this corpse of light.

Back in the shack, a glass of water overturned on the floor spread out and evaporated before we could move to wipe the spot, leaving a dark stain on the boards. Not enough for a fly to drink.

The flies wanted something else: they hung in midair or dropped suddenly on to an arm or leg, insensible of danger, ignoring the hand raised against them. It's our sticky selves they desire, taste of sweat and salt, the rich bitter blood. I slapped a fat one that grazed along my shoulder. He fell out of the air stupefied, half dead already, slowly turning wing over wing in hallucinatory mirage currents of heat. I wandered from bunk to window frame, lay down and stared up at the ceiling, scratched at a great bite on my thigh until it opened; a splash of alcohol there, and I winced and swore as it seethed through my cells. Time simply passed; the earth turned slowly, and we rode it around with the patience born of having no choice. You couldn't call it waiting exactly—the way waiting points forward, directed outside the moment—rather we remained, hot, heavy, and yes, patient, riding inside time. Bert squatted on the porch in a slab of shadow, scratched a reed pen over worked and reworked lines of a drawing, connecting certain marks and pressing others back into oblivion. Crouched there on his haunches, he looked for all the world like some old savage, drawing the four directions with a stick in the dirt. I stared at my hands, turning them over and back, tracking alluvial cracks the sun made translucent, feeling the blood swell in my fingertips, stalled, lingering, before it was pushed back through the blue wrist vein. I stared at the white chips of my nails as if the faintest coolness was coming off their hard surfaces; I stared, allowing my eyes to rest on the nearest thing and slowly divine its contours. The thing might have been a tabletop or the view from a window, but because I was lying down it was not, it was only my hand against the red bedcover and I stared at it as if it were not mine, as if I could be far away or someone else and when that did not work I got up and drank a cup of cold, iron-flavored water and heard again the terns crying below on the beach, a sound which had continued to rise and fall even though for a while I had stopped hearing it.

Now toward evening a redwing shrills from the weathervane. A sparrow chirps busily in the tangled bay and poison ivy outside the window, rattling the branches to stir up a small breeze. Within the shadow of deep grass a toad pants. Light clouds pushed out of the east give the sky new depth, breaking up that unrelieved glare of midday, and the waves turn over with a gratified sigh. I go out on the deck and look out. Far out a boat horn speaks deeply; now grass moves, and unmoving branches, dead sticks with no green, darken slightly, pulling a new dampness from the air. They may not be quite dead; they may be wanting to put out leaves, or to hold on until the world moves again under them.

The horses come down the beach, mounted by unschooled riders, following single file behind the leader. From far off only their movement stands out, that up and down canter as they cross below, while the bumpy shape of a large boat offshore seems not to be moving at all until I turn back and the horizon is empty.

It is evening coming, and rain coming on. Behind these first puffy clouds a phalanx of low dark ones frowns on the horizon, gathering force, and the northeast breeze blown ahead of them feels wet and cool. This wind carries water and oxygen to quicken the world, freshening cells of leaf and hill. A breeze blows across the chipped waves. Each wave that breaks sprays particles of seawater up into the air; as the wind carries them inland we taste salt.

Blackbirds are massing on the next hill, making chittery, tossing flights, settling down and rising up again in annoyance. Down on the beach the gulls circle and float in broad ellipses. There is a general rising and falling: leaves flip on the branches, grasstops shake, and towels fly up on the line. My hair whips into my face; the wind pulls it straight back, then everything sags and settles.

The air smells of wind and pepper; the birds' voices are shrill as they swoop back and forth, and light flutters on the grass, showing silver, then deep green. All along the foredune the grass is bent before the wind's motion. The shack stands to take the measure and shape of the wind pushing at it. One has to give, and for now the wind divides. Sand dances in short leaps inches off the ground, each grain landing to dislodge the next, making dust clouds along the tops of the dunes. Skeins of sand whirl down the slope of the nearest big dune, twisting and twirling. The beach roses in front of the shack look surprised, their branches flailing the air, as the wind pushes the ground away beneath them, grain by grain, persuading the multitudes singly, a force no force can halt.

But now it seems to stop. Grass luffs in the dying breeze and a cool dampness settles over the valley. In the quiet a bobwhite repeats his urgent greeting, saying hopefully it is not too late.

I walk across the ridge and down into the valley by the pump. The sky turns light grey, seeming to absorb the cloud shapes that dashed across it, and the horizon darkens as wind flails the grass and disappears. I can't tell if the wetness beading my arms is sweat or mist, if this air grows heavy with rain or fire.

The blackbirds have left the bayberry. Beside the pump the

huge bush is dark and silent; no alarm sounds at my approach. For weeks they danced and called and flew in circles over our heads when we appeared at the top of the path. The male whistled and flew around us, while she fled to a nearby bush crying help. He fluttered, she moaned, all the while we pumped the buckets full and tugged them uphill, feeling guilty and harassed.

But yesterday all that was over. The pair flew past us unconcerned, as if nothing marked that spot, once so hotly defended.

Perhaps the nestlings have fledged and flown, but I suspect disaster: the marsh hawk. She has been around all week, raising panic in the valley every evening as she hunts along the ground and beats the grass for signs of life. I approach the bayberry cautiously, but nothing happens. I circle the bush, twelve feet across, looking for the well-hidden nest, but I see only tangles, thorns, and a deepening dark within. It is so quiet down here. Up above me, over the hill, the whole gang of blackbirds flies about full of weather news and excitement, swooping and calling back and forth.

The first drops make small depressions in the sand, and the sand begins to give up the heat borne down on it all day. A reversal is beginning: the earth's warmth will go back up into the sky and the sky will let go cool drops into the sun-warmed earth. This afternoon animals hid in the shade; now they will come out. Rain cools the hissing fringes of the waves. Darkness begins to contract horizons; I stare hard at what is near, shifting into shadow: twigs and branches, the scuffed depressions in the sand where we have walked back and forth, a darkening stalk of high grass. Branches and leaves become one mass as the ground rises into them; backlighting gives shape to taller grasses, detail lost, the ground all one color. The rain still holds back, letting go in fat drops, a few here and there; you can walk between them.

As simply as that, the rain hitting my face, standing below the hill in the open, the change happened. I felt it like a gear slipping into place. A muscle relaxing across my shoulder, the board sliding into the notch, giving room to move without constraint. As the rain fell into the earth which pulls everything to itself, it seemed all space fell into order, pulling me with it. Clouds gathered weight and broke, falling into the earth, to lie upon the leaves and strike the bare hills, to break over our heads. And I stand here among birds and blowing grasses, adding my mass to that summoning, part of the storm falling towards me, falling as the earth falls, forward, circling back.

I stood there below the hill, feeling the beating of my chest against the air. Then I looked up and got my breath pulled out of my throat. A crowd of gulls was passing overhead, flying back into the dunes as they do every evening. White and dark, they take the wind under them, moaning as they leave the beach, flocking up to the slopes where they sit in disgruntled company on the sand, all facing one direction. Tonight though, with the light on their backs, against the darkening east, they seem strange, more than themselves.

Tonight they touch the outlines of the timeless. Black against a pale, curdling sky, they cross the sky in whirling spirals. In their passing are one thousand thousand summer evenings. They fly into the gathering storm, light glancing on their wings, the black, winged ones, shapes that cross the earth at night. Touched by those shadows I turn invisible. They have always been here and my life is so brief. I stand in the open and watch them come, flexed, wing against wing, above the wind-furrowed grass, as they fly back into the dunes, swirling down to disappear behind the hill where storm clouds are massing.

For an instant I seemed to remember something I'd been trying to say for a long time, something I knew, but did not fully understand until that moment—then that low, mumbling chorus overtook me. And then there was nothing left in me to think it. I was flown through, emptied and taken back. When I came back to myself I knew that I had been lifted, not in joy but in dread, and I knew that it did not matter. Raised up by the black wings or the white, you're equally gone, emptied. And then there is no remembering and no question.

I'm left here. Shake it off and turn back. Climb the hill and look out over the horizon. Now the rain breaks in ribbons driven sideways into my face, and a storm wind keens across the emptied landscape. I turn toward the shack, walk a few steps, then begin to run.

An eerie darkness is gathering over Euphoria. Thunder rumbles across the waves and the sky turns weirdly stark and violent; the walls shake in sympathy. I close the door with difficulty, leaning on the wind to ease the wood over the swollen sill. The big board falls tight into its latch across the door frame. Then the room is small and filled with us.

Cold now in my summer dress, my skin wet, goosebumps rising along my arms, I go to stand next to Bert. He takes me under his arm, inside the thick shadow of his shoulder, his body's heat. We watch together from our window as the combers fume and churn and plow up on shore.

We light the stove and set out lamps, confident in our small shelter, as the storm sweeps down on the land. Fill the lamps and check the water supply, eight buckets full, count our store of batteries for flashlight and radio, put out candles. Make everything tight and ready. We'll keep an ear on the weather station just to be safe—though it's not yet hurricane season. Hazel has left us a red flag to fly from the roof as a distress signal—but who would see it here? If a hurricane were forecast, we'd shutter the windows, unhook the propane tanks, and try to get out. Euphoria would likely stand as she has before, but the wind could shatter glass; a fuel tank toppled over could ignite.

Dark closes fast now, rain pelting the windows. For dinner we choose something from our store of cans and it is wonderful, miraculous that someone put this food into a can—beef stew, as it happens—that someone prepared it for us. Clear water in the pan, rice measured out; we'll ladle the stew over it as night comes down and the tide leaps up the beach. Wind luffs the sides of the shack, bursts of rain, and then the warm stillness flowing back. Rice grains rattle in the tin; they scratch as I stir them into the water. Whoosh of the can opener biting into the lip, grinding metal teeth around the sealed diameter. We are rich and wise, in possession of metal tools, fire, shelter and light. Cooked food, and blankets folded across the beds. For thousands of years we have sought this shelter. In tents or houses, in walled fortresses or circles of wooden huts where the fire crouched, smoke seeping into the breath and bones of the people. For thousands of years we have spoken to each other in the hush of coming storms, passing pots back and forth, drawing near the fire. I slice crusty bread as Bert pours water into the basin; the lampglow shines in his eyes. Beyond his watching face, his spirit watches.

We wash the dishes by lamplight, using as little water as we can manage. I sweep the floor and tidy up in the first burst of energy in days, folding and stacking towels rescued from the line, clearing tables of books and papers. We lean together beside a lamp to take up the endless game of gin rummy, slap the cards down, add up the points in the summer's tally. Wind tests the cracks, bursts of rain rocking us, and then stillness—it's still coming.

The storm picks up again with a gash of light and a sickening thud as thunder hits the hill behind us. The shack shakes from roof to floorboards, down through the underpinnings, then rain gushes down with a sudden release and blows in sheets against the windows. It is a rolling, summer storm, a real Cape Cod tempest. The air crackles with static. Nothing comes through on the radio. Then a giant spark rips down the sky, white light slashes across the room followed by a violet strobe.

We stand stock-still in the middle of the room, pulled to our feet as lightning rips open a landscape rendered bright and flat as nightmare. A flash, a print on the retina, and in the swift dark the dying rumble of thunder subsiding, rolling over, like furniture dragged across a floor. The vision given by lightning is too quick; it reaches the brain just as darkness closes back in. We see a landscape of memory, lingering for moments on the back of the brain. The shack jerks and rocks as lightning shoots down; the world disappears and reappears, time seems to stop: the water is lit up bright and flat as an electric sheet and the dunes rise up in their Egyptian stillness.

We stand, surrounded by wind, inside the shack that trembles with its fury. The stovepipe beats back and forth, shaking down a black rain of fat sooty drops, and rain is driven down inexhaustibly, running over the sides of the shack. We hold on to one another, transfixed, as Euphoria sails into the storm.

TWENTY

Staying In

Morning. The storm has passed and left behind a steady rain that promises to pour down on us for days. The wind bangs the shack like a wooden gong and glass rattles in the window frames. There is no going out: it's given that we will stay inside, listening to the rain beat the walls, occasional thunder growling up. The temperature has fallen thirty degrees and streams of water shove under the door; we put down newspapers, then towels, until everything is soaked and the smell of wet newsprint clings in our nostrils. We wear all our clothes, sweatshirts and jeans and sweaters, in layers mismatched and lumpy. There's no dry firewood; the gas stove boils water for tea. No fire, tea and crackers, and wearing all our clothes.

Afternoon. We rested and read all morning, tired after a sleepless night. I tried to get out a little bit during a seeming lull, but the rain soaked me through, and when I came back it was hard to get warm again, with tea and blankets and my last dry socks. The windows press fog and mist and we are cut off, adrift in the grey, beating rain.

We take up a lot of room, suddenly large as we move around the shack. I feel dangerously shut in, blinded by the closed door and rain-soaked windows. To go from the table to the cupboard I must displace Bert, who is sitting on a camp chair beside the cold stove. To make a third cup of tea, Bert has to get past me at the table; if he wants to sit there too I have to get up and pull out the bench, and move books and papers, cups and spoons out of his way. We maintain an elaborate courtesy. I think of old hut dwellers who would live like this whole winters. The smell of smoke and stale bodies, wet socks, and the fear of going mad. I fall asleep in self-defense, a stale, unrestful sleep, visited by dreams of giants.

For lunch I make a pot of soup, using the last of the potatoes and onions, some sausage and dry milk. When the wind turns we get an occasional patch of radio. A station somewhere in Maine is playing all the songs of 1958 from two o'clock to three-thirty. "Davy Crockett, King of the Wild Frontier," leads off. I count the hours until supper. If we were in town today, we would go to the movies or sit in a bar with friends . . .

Second morning. Last night it was hard to sleep because we hadn't moved all day. I lay in my bunk and heard the rain beat only inches over my head, its mental chatter like the details of many lives dropping singly and together. Outside, each creature crouched in its shelter: the owl, the hawk, the tidy, plush bodies of mouse and mole. Nothing was hunting or hunted; every beast and fowl and creeping thing was gathered into its place. What were the terns doing? The adults leave the nest to ride out the storm on the waves, but how were the chicks surviving? Could they last a second night in this heavy rain, with nothing to protect them—or had the storm tide already washed them out? Lying there I imagined scenes of desolation. Shipwrecked sailors wandering the dark, how long a man might search for shelter here. Bert began snoring then in fitful bursts, as irritating a sound as you could possibly imagine, and louder than the rain.

We woke to find the door still leaking. This was not amusing. The boards are soaked through now, and along the back wall a thin stream of water courses downward, winding past the window-frame and across the floor where it drips out through cracks in the boards. The wind shudders and pushes, body of wind, big shoulder heaved at the walls. We can see nothing from the windows; the shack is cold as a tomb, wreathed in cloud. Shut inside, we glare at each other over tea. I sit in bed with my journal and find I have no thoughts. Words advance across the page in merciless progression; sentence follows sentence, idea flows out of observation, words putting out more words and none of it means anything to me today. The pages feel thick and soft in my hands. We lie on the beds and read, or dial the radio across the numbers of distant cities. Voices scratch out of the metal box like a needle pulled across grooves.

Afternoon. My book this week is peopled with characters suffering from bad marriages and too much gin—it seemed witty enough on a bright, noisy day when I borrowed it from a friend in town. We eat an endless bowl of soup, dipping out of the pot that never diminishes. We start to hate the soup. I make another pot of tea; the crackers are stale and damp. This matters more than either of us could have imagined. The rain persists. Bert says he'll take a walk anyway; I say he might as well swim in a whirlpool. He comes back quickly and spreads wet sheets of clothing over chairs and I only just mention having told him so. We play scrabble. We play gin rummy, peeling the cards up from the soft, fibrous wood. Bert's raincoat hangs on a chair like a dejected visitor, melting into a pool on the floor. We move our chairs to the furthest corners and plan separate vacations. The wind makes the most godawful noises. Arias and death-cries, keening and barking, terrible scrapings and thunder of something falling over. It shakes the walls to get our attention but when I listen it still doesn't make sense.

"Do you realize that when Picasso was my age he had already invented and discarded Cubism?" Bert says, looking up from his sketchbook.

"Picasso was a shit," I tell him.

"Maybe you *have* to be a shit to get anywhere. Be selfish, just live in the work. Let somebody else clean up." He pauses. "I don't know if it's healthy for an artist to be in a relationship."

I ignore this last. "Well, when Keats was my age he was already dead."

"Why do you always have to make it be about you?"

Time grinds to a stunning halt after this exchange; we're quiet and glum, padding about in our socks and long underwear, feeling snappish. Why do I live with this hulking, hairy, stale-smelling, large and surly creature? We turn on the news and get a weak signal, then static: the batteries are failing. We're cut off from the world: does no one think of us, or care to ask how we survive? Boredom relives boredom, running mental films of random action, exhausting with its she said and then that happened, how it all comes to nothing. Stand in the middle of the room and listen: the afternoon seems tranquilized, spent of passion, gently breathing. Then a quick blast throws a truckload of sand at the walls and the shack staggers, sways, and rights itself.

Night. This night comes early, black night in which everything disappears. Then wind, thunder again—it's hard to believe no one's angry. What does the air hit to make it stop so suddenly? A light sways violently offshore, then light opens into light; the waters sheen electric pale. The shack trembles like an animal that smells fire. Tucked up in blankets, not really warm, I fall asleep feeling sorry for all of us.

Shadows pile up at the door. Ghosts of lost creatures, sailors, ancestors, all I have tried to put away from me here, cry out, demanding comfort. Go away. Get on, you storm voices, you mysteries, leave me alone, you damned lost endless multitudes, and the hell with you. Where you come from there are more of you, endless you's, the centrifugal force of your woes pulling me toward you, and I will not go. I do not want to go with you because I know you are dead. A shadow stands on the doorstep, rain pasting his clothes to his body, his hair slapped to his forehead, a streaming wraith wrung out in the sea's agitation, with the deadlight shining in his eyes. His silence is a demand; he says nothing. If I bring you into my bed to warm you you still are dead and I am cold from holding you. No—you nothings, you dead voices, you windborne sorrows, no to you.

In my dream a lamb roast is turning on a spit; tents billow in gaudy colors across a desert camp. I dream the elders are gathering, caravans arriving by day and night, and the lamb turns on the spit, its skin splitting, black char of fat and the head revolves over and around, righted and spun downward, staring from burnt eye-sockets. Meat, hot and running with fat, savory with herbs, the smell of the animal growing stronger in the fire.

In the dark a skunk comes knocking, treading up the path, wet fur effusing skunk stink. I wake and taste it in the back of my throat, through my sinuses, inside my lungs. He bangs once at the trash can and pads off. I wait, listening. The rain has stopped. I listen some more, then get up and open the door.

The quietest night, weighted with damp, lies on the world. A faint glow of moonlight burnishes the clouds, and night sleeps. It is right to say the storm has lifted; I can feel the air spring back under it, the grasses uncoiling. There is the blink off and on, around and back, of Highland Light, not visible for days.

The stairs hang down like a bridge between lives; a soft radiance is on the sand. Grasses bend seed plumes toward the flowing dunes, their lapped curves standing still a moment in their constant retreat. Offshore, boats circle their anchors, afloat on the consciousness of water, and the moonlight wakes a struggle of roses gripped down in sand. Their blossoms clenched tight, roots pulling hard to earth, they bury themselves holding on. Behind

TWENTY-ONE

Fishers

In first light the earth wears its eternal body: each shape of brush and leaf is fixed and still, the shoreline joined to the water at every turn. Light filters out of the sky, soft and grainy, touching every grass and woody twig, the undersides of leaves, with the exact form of their separate being. The air is cool and damp. The only motion is the slow drift of clouds off to the southwest. From the doorstep I hear one bird call, a single note rising up from the valley. The screen door creaks, its damp complaint of steel against swollen wood, and the rusted spring tugs inward with a sleepy sound. Behind me the room floats in shadow. Bert turns and sighs, exhaling stale breaths of sleep; I hesitate, then quickly pull on shorts and a t-shirt, and walk out into the dense, salt-laden air.

Wet grasses touch my legs as I climb the hill. The roses are furled, pouting on their stems, their soft, dark emerald leaves crumpled around them. A cloud of midges swims in the air, doing their atom dance, electrons defining an empty center. Bred out of thin air, they hover in the currents of my breath and my blood's rich tropical climate; I wave my arm and a vortex of glittering motes swirls after, drawn in the wake of body heat. At the crest of the hill the foredune falls away toward the beach in a slope of long grasses, softly bent, no light or motion in them yet. *Ammophilia*: "sand lover." The grass is dotted with little purple flowers of beach me, the shack is dark as a shell; the whisper of surf breaking on the beach below is like the jet stream around a disappearing space craft. The shack rises up behind me. Sheer and hollow, wingless, it rises as the ground flows out beneath it. I am standing here on the night earth on my two white legs, on moving ground, out here awake in the moonlight, not dreaming, alive in the dark before naming.

pea, and seaside goldenrod, still green and nubby on the stems. The grass, too, is a flower, stalk on stalk of minutest blossoms, seed-sparks clustered at the head.

Dawn unfolds gradually: first a decomposition of the dark and then a slow reassertion of forms. Day does not break, but unfurls in a steady gesture, opening from within. Clouds on the horizon fume and swell, and now the sun floats up out of the sea, shoots its red rays sideways, and disappears into a bank of clouds. The gulls wheel toward it, crying as if the sun had never been seen before, and all along the foredune the grasses toss and shake the wet from their heads. The world shivers in a membrane of light, cold and tender. A shell blue sky opens above the horizon, holding a piece of moon as thin as skin.

My appearance at the top of the path seems to have wakened the terns over to the east, who rise up and circle over their nests, flashing white wings and pointy tails, and screeking out dire warnings. Bright chips of white, their black caps making sharp accents, they flash and cry at the waves and the gulls and at each other.

The wet sand sticks to my feet in clumps, coarse grains giving way in great deep prints. Each grain holds its separate cushion of moisture, each a distinct planet pushed apart by the water's pressure. An outgoing tide has swept the beach clean, lifting sticks and bottles and shells, and dry, snarled mats of seaweed in its flood. The sand is smooth and untracked, with objects simply laid across its surface, as if placed there by extraterrestrials. A red buoy, a mayonnaise jar, bits of shipwood and fishnet, all lie as if on display. Down at the waterline, pieces of jellyfish dot the sand; pink, purple, lavender, they quiver with a touch, all protoplasm and water. Fish eggs and dead legs of crab. There's a goose, a flock of anxious sanderlings, and a big black crow picking his way among the rubble like a pharaoh. The body of a great black-backed gull lies up on the berm, his beak stuck straight into the sand bank, looking as if he had just fallen over in mid-step. One clear eye gazes up at the sky and his wings are flung outward slightly, as if to check a fall. A piping plover darts past, sprinting in and out of the tracks, pecking at wrack and seaweed, disappearing against the sand, then popping back into view. Sparrow-sized, the color of dry sand, he looks wonderfully neat and serious. He passes the dead gull without pausing, truly unaware of the presence of death. He runs past me and stops to squat as if on a nest, peeps sweetly in a worried tone, then leaves it and runs again, and squats; he's leading me away from his brood, he thinks. It's worth the effort, good for a try; it's what he knows how to do.

A lot of the rubbish on the beach this morning has washed off fishing boats. I spot a gobstick lying clean up on the sand—a wooden bat about eighteen inches long the fishermen use to clobber the big fish they heave up on board. It's heavy, weighted at one end, with a worn leather thong for a handle. I pick it up and swing it at my side as I stride along, liking the feel of its weight, the way it fits my hand. Smooth, well-balanced, meant to swing through the air and come down hard, it has the satisfying feel of something made and useful, a patina of old use smoothing its grain. To club them—a kindness, I suppose. These items of industry are strangely cheering, these lines and nets tangled and looped with seaweed, these painted buoys, even this murder weapon of a bat—they have a reason to be here, a serious intent in the scheme of things. They seem as natural as fish-heads, or the jingle shells sucked out by moon snails, that chatter back and forth at the tide line.

A truck festooned with fishing poles, buckets dancing off the back, rounds the bend from Race Point and rolls toward me, bouncing in the ruts. It passes beneath the berm, hugging the firm sand at the tide line, heading home at dawn. I turn my head to wave and the driver raises one hand carefully from the wheel. A little blond-haired boy lies sleeping across his chest.

They would have come out some time after midnight to get the best of the night fishing, and to be here for that hour just before dawn when the fish feed best. When I rolled over, hearing Bert's slow, heavy breathing, as the tide reached its fullest point, hesitated, and fell back, when I sat up, sensing the darkness breaking up, they were already out. Before dawn and through the morning's run, while the water simmered steel grey and churned with life, I was just stirring, turning over in my bed, and they stood in the waves and cast and pulled back, the man and the boy beside him.

It's getting to be a good time for stripers; every night we see lights of jeeps parked down at the shoreline, and dark figures casting into the shadows. Bluefish have been running since June. Now that the terns and plovers have hatched out, parts of the beach are opened to traffic; there's a lumbering parade of jeeps and pickups down from Snail Road most every day.

The fishermen are the most constant visitors here. They come on grey days and at odd hours, following an almanac of tide, currents, and rumor rather than the weather reports dispensed by the Chamber of Commerce. They come at dusk and stand peering into the surf, while the tide presses in and out ahead of them. They stand for hours at the water's edge, casting, sticking their rods into the sand to wait for a strike, then reeling in to cast again. Even at a distance it is clear what they are after, how they stand up before the whole Atlantic in readiness, in attendance on ordinary wonders, keeping strange hours, and faith in the plain, possible miracle of fish. Their darkening forms grow heavy as night falls, as they stand half in the water in hip boots, there where the world falls off. These are "ordinary men out of the ordinary," someone once said, released from the narrow, nagging world into a wide and mysterious landscape. In the morning their wheel ruts bruise the sand and their bootprints swell like the tracks of an enormous vanished race.

They want something, and this makes them peaceful. They want fish and know their chances, so they wait.

You stay still and listen, alert for a tug of line or any disturbance in the water, but meanwhile there are the stars, and the sand cooling, and the weird cries the seagulls make just before dawn. You stand watching lights moving slowly offshore, under the great moving lights of the Big Dipper, rotated clockwise around the axis of the north star. Your life is with you and not with you then—you stand in the time of hours, of things like tides, and phases of the moon, but also somehow inside or next to the endlessness of these, knowing in your cells that what the tide perpetually measures is nothing, and you pull in the fish and the sea is still not empty and you are satisfied with it or not, with the water washing over your feet. The fish is alive, you see it for a minute, then it dies and becomes food. This wanting is endless, a kind of elemental greed that keeps replenishing itself like any hunger, taking the world in constantly through its single need.

More distant, and strangely heroic, are those ones who sail out after the fish, whose lives are spent at sea, dragging offshore or fishing the dangerous ledges of Georges Bank. I see them beyond our window, heading out to sea where they crank up heavy nets in the cold, the water streaming through the mesh that strains with the bodies of fish. They go out by necessity, putting the same question to the sea over and over. Each time, the answer the sea gives is inarguable. I have seen them returning to the town pier in the purple November twilight, off-loading fish with meat-red hands and wool hats pulled low on their foreheads. I see them in the mornings from my window, headed east, and sometimes at night floating out past the bars with a single light hung up on their masts. "Viaha com Deus," the Portuguese captains say, "Go with God," as they cast off. Little Natalia, Gale Winds, Liberty Belle, Jimmy Boy, Little Infant, Carla B., Second Effort: the names painted along the bows reach for luck or adventure, or celebrate family, wives, partners. There are Silver Mink, Plymouth

Belle, Alwa, North Star, Pauly B. The names are for remembering. I think of the Captain Bill, which went down my first winter here, drowning all hands. How many others before, all wrecked, broken up, their crews lost? Sea full of fish: the sea will feed you, swallow your bones. Still the Charlotte G., Ancora Praia, Pat Sea, Chico and Jess, go out from the pier with full crews. In the nets the bones are hauled in, the dead and the living picked from the moving current, and the decks are piled with silver, glistening bodies, the smell of blood and salt in them, cold, shimmering wet-eyed, bright-scaled, firm-fleshed fishes thumping the decks.

The fish are a gift: vital, immaculate bodies of streaming light, each one a shining fire. Cod, mackerel, minnows and bass, bluefish and tuna (called "horse mackerel" by the early settlers who would only use it for fertilizer), flounder, skate, and squid, and shark: the fish are strangers, citizens of another realm. They live inside shifting currents, always moving ahead and sideways, wriggling and darting, or they hang suspended in water, slowly flapping their fins against the current. Slippery fellows, queerest of folk, the fish is a gift, the fish is a mystery, the fish is food, who knows what a fish is?

Torpedo shaped, lacking limbs, they propel themselves forward by weaving movements, working side to side against the force of the water they must feel touching them always, heavier, denser than the air we know, more real. Cold-blooded, the oldest vertebrates, they are twenty thousand species, in fresh and salt water. They go by singly and in rushing schools, following light, prey, and flowing currents. They strand themselves following some necessity onto shore; they leap up in the water, slip and flash, breaking the surface, panicked by feeding schools below, some powerfully muscled, some mere slivers of light. The fish disappear under tons of water into the dark below, and tons of fish are hauled out of the waves, squirming and heaving, smacking the wet decks, violent with savage power.

We use fish to catch fish, an imitative magic, turning their hunger back against them. We catch them by the mouth, by their hunger, their open-jawed need, and haul them in on lines where they thrash and flail and bite the air. Fish are hauled out of dark water into the glare of headlights—their last vision is of blinding light on a dry, unbreathable shore. We catch fish in nets, in waving filaments that take the shape of water, that billow and waver like water weeds or tendrils of shadow. Gulls follow the boats, rolling and screaming as the nets are pulled in, birds of pure voracious appetite, holding the reflection of the sea in their eyes.

The clamor of the terns increases as I walk along, cutting just below their colony. A few birds make threatening sweeps at my head as they fly over. I wonder how they're doing since the storm. There are chicks running back and forth, and parents feeding them, but it's hard to judge the population without going in there and counting, which I will not do. All their effort is bent at driving off intruders and it seems the least favor to leave them well alone. They endure gale winds, rain and sun, jeep traffic, and attacks by hawks, foxes, gulls and owls, to raise their young on this strip of sand, riding the waves offshore when storms lash the beach, fleeing under the shadow of the great horned owl, and returning to meet the morning with a shrill hunger, crying and wheeling after fish. All day we glimpse them in the distance, at the edge of our vision, hovering over the water with fast, shallow wing-beats. They drop into the waves with their bills pointing down, and climb the air, catching a rising current, and the tide circles gracefully to turn and return, bringing squid and schools of sand eels, crabs, and small fish into the shallows.

Down in front of Frenchie's shack a little motorboat has fetched up on shore, where it sits half in and half out of the water, snagged on a sandbank, swaying mildly in the current. It must have broken its mooring and washed down from Chatham or Orleans, to float up here onto the bars. The park rangers will notify police down cape this morning and somebody will come and claim it, tow it home, little runaway.

The little boat bounces in the ebbs and swells. I walk along swinging the bat against my thigh, keeping time. When I get closer I see that it is intact, though swamped. It is a small boat, comfortable for three or four people, its red plastic cushions hanging down at funny angles. I feel an urge to replace them, and I do, and then I get in and sit down, my feet in three inches of water, settle the bat across my knees, and face out to sea.

The terns fly busily back and forth overhead, satisfied to ignore me now that I have settled on my own business and none of theirs. I sit by the water's edge, rocking, as little waves break and slosh up the sides of the boat. Waves drag stones back and forth on the bottom. Should I be a fisher? Set sail, cast out a line over the water? It's a fine morning for starting out. High, clean winds and open skyways ahead. My eyes follow a shadow of fins underwater, a slick on the surface, a cloud of gulls far out. The terns flash and plummet into the swirling surf. Shrill and driven by necessity, with a wild bright hunger, life spends itself constantly. The world moves forward in great circles, following ancient, wide-armed lines of regeneration. These currents do not fail—wind and tide, fish and gull, the sandpipers running up and down the beach with their insatiable, panicked appetites.

The fishermen have gone home to sleep. The boy, rolled into bed without waking, floats in the rocking tide of first slumber, deep grooves of memory settling in his brain, the memory of waves splashing up, the truck rocking side to side. Back up the hill, the shack will be still and quiet; Bert may be turning over, sliding deeper into the covers, the dim light gathering around his face. I'm hungry too, and wanting company. I think I'll head back, maybe fry a few eggs, wake him up.

August

Since i have been walking back and forth to town to work every day mon through fridays and sometimes on sat, i have, each time i have come upon fresh deer tracks, told Sal about it . . . these fresh tracks always excite me in the sense that, as i walk to work over the dunes through town, i know, when i see them, that the deer have made the tracks just an hour or so, or sometimes, minutes before me.

—CHARLIE SCHMID ("Dune Charlie")
Excerpt from a journal

TWENTY-TWO

Meridian

Now it is August and the days are slow. We're strong and lazy, fed up on sweetness and the fat of the land. Chores slip from our hands as we linger at summer's table, talking quietly over coffee, extending every pleasure as the season burnishes to gold.

In town the guest houses and restaurants are full: "No Vacancy" declares itself from every window. Traffic moves sluggishly as Route Six bloats like a python that has swallowed a springbok. Cars wait at the bridges, squeezed forward by the peristaltic pressure of rotaries. Now tourists and townspeople troop out to the beach all day—hikers, jeep picnickers, fishermen, swimmers and sunbathers. Yesterday a group of teenagers trying to be human kites flew dangling from winged harnesses, eight feet off the ground, pulled in turn behind a fat-wheeled pickup. The girls' shrieks rose over the snarl of the truck's wheels grubbing down in sand, sending mingled sounds of pleasure and gasoline engines floating up the hill. We lounged on the deck in afternoon shadow. A purple balloon wafted overhead, blown from the public beach at Race Point, two miles west.

Flies hang by the door all day, stupidly content. In July we slapped them down, hunted each one vigorously to its death. But now we wave them away, show them the door, the hell with them. They go slowly, fat and dirty and unafraid, herded from the door they will never leave, where they wait endlessly to be let in or out, buzzing lazily in the key of F.

Back among the dunes, high-bush blueberries the size of BBs hang in a dusky haze over bogs presided over by jays and mockingbirds. Mosquitoes swim in the air with vicious, prayerful whispers, fainting on a breath of insect repellent, but returning to float just out of reach, failing again and returning. Underfoot, cranberries store up their sweetness, beginning to show red. August sees little new growth, but a fulfillment of forms, as fruits ripen slowly from within, swelling and hardening, elaborating each cell in the long, generous light of late summer. Gardeners call this "sitting time," these hot, humid days when things come simply into their own. Now as the sun works through the flesh, the world waits and does nothing, becoming ever more fully itself. And don't tell me you are tired of summer. It isn't true. It isn't possible. Perfect ripe tomatoes falling in wet slices across the plate. A sky like this.

We wake in the same small room to the sound of waves, butter our toast at the table and hurry down to the beach. The morning's chores will wait, but this particular slant of light, this slightest breeze whispered up from the south, smelling of grass and sun-warmed sand—these won't come again.

This morning high winds had buffed the sky up to a clear, Chinese turquoise, with not a cloud to set it off, a sky you might go and live in. Down here at eye level not a breeze moved. The water sloshed gently up onto the sand, splashing over our feet as we walked into it and out again. A white motorboat cut in close to the beach with a sawing noise, its prow spanking up and down in the surf. Sand flies rose up at our ankles, murmuring lasciviously.

We walked east toward Thalassa, where two generations of park service signs guarded the tern colony: the old "Nesting Terns: Keep Out" notice superseded by a later warning that read: "Caution: Young Birds in Tracks." Now the nests are empty, the colony has scattered, and sand forms little mounds at the base of each signpost—a line of wooden poles staggering off into the distance. The citizenry appeared calm, ignoring us as we tracked the water's edge. The birds still gave their high, shrill cries from time to time, flying back and forth across the water, but they have lost their accusing tone and seem addressed less to any mortal than to the elements themselves and to the shimmering landscape. These are leisurely days for them, a pause between the anxious work of nesting and the long flight back to South America. They inhabit this time easily, swooping overhead, making little chases back and forth—perhaps youngsters practicing their dives—seeming, briefly, willing to be a part of this scene, instead of constantly protesting their condition.

There is a fullness on the land these days, a saturation of light and a feeling of calm. I saw the marsh hawk this morning, but the tree swallows have flown away and the song sparrow is unnaturally quiet. The red-winged blackbirds have disappeared en masse, keeping out of sight in the marshes while they go through their molt. They won't be seen again until September, when they reemerge to form huge flocks before starting their migration south. Mama and two young sanderlings, picking along the strand, seemed not in a hurry for once, world enough and time.

We walked the beach quietly, steeped in our interior rhythms. Our progress was halted every few yards as Bert stopped to pick up the most unlikely objects, turning each one over in his hands with a wondering look, as if he had never seen such things before. Mermaid's purses, odd bits of frosted sea glass, sand dollars with incised patterns of stars; he would inspect each find closely before placing it in his pocket or casting it aside.

A whelk's egg case lay tangled in a heap of eelgrass, alongside a particularly loathsome spider crab, recently deceased and already beginning to stink. The crab's toad-shaped body and long scrawny legs were coated with sea-moss, a diatomaceous ooze housing algae and tube worms: at its best the creature was always hideous. Bert bent down and carefully disentangled from this mess a string of parchment discs a foot and a half long. Nearly weightless, it formed a continuous loop like a corkscrew, wafting in the air, translucent and fragile as old parchment—a made thing of another realm. He shook it lightly and a sound as soft as sand grains fluttered down its length, the shells of hundred of tiny, dead whelks shifted through endless compartments making a dry shushing sound like rain.

Bert goes out into the dunes every morning, moving through the landscape with a pen and a sketchpad. He's just finished the piece he's been building since spring. The reed is stiff now, bleached to a hay color, and the driftwood poles have given up all their sea-dampness to the air; they stand white as bones. He can't add anything now; the materials resist any change. He's taking photographs, the only record that will remain when the piece is taken down.

Yesterday he returned to say he had named the piece: "Secret." Naming always comes last: now it exists for itself, taking its place among the pines and undergrowth, in the intimate space of the bog as the season completes its business around it.

On my best days I can sit for hours at my desk. Draft upon draft, the poems grow and are cut back, change and turn, pulling me with them. The pleasure is in giving myself over to it, to lose the consciousness of any distance between myself and the work. I answer to nothing and no one here, forgetting the world entirely in these hours. This is not the work of production, or even the dutiful pleasure of chores, but a devotion to something larger than I can ever achieve. A poem may be finished, in time, but the work cannot, must not, be finished. To be "finished" in that sense, would be to fail. "She's finished," they say when inspiration has fled, and not in congratulation.

Much of what I love about this place is the concentration it allows. In the silence, thoughts and images are intensified, distilled like salt from seawater. To meet the great, shining surface of the beach and the vault of sky over sand and water, to be a single particle in all that space, and then to return to the small interior of the shack and hold all that inside me—this is a weighty pleasure.

Bert's methods are different. He moves through the world, measuring space with his body. The walk across the dunes is part of it, the sky and wind, the smell of the hot sand. He sits and draws in a windbreak, his back against a wall of sand, staying away for hours.

Sometimes I envy the activity of his work, how he uses all his senses and his body. This lack of separation between self and world intrigues me, though I'd never be capable of it. When he draws in the afternoons in the shack he likes the radio on, letting music or baseball scores accompany his moving hand. He seems to let sound, landscape, sense impressions, flow through him as he works. I cannot write to any voice beside my own, or follow any language but the sentences spinning out of my own head. I sit at a table with my back to the water, my head down, block out the world and build it all again.

Morning catches a rhythm, builds and crests, and slowly recedes. Bert returns to find me gathering my papers into a pile, sweeping the tabletop clean. Was anything accomplished? I'll leave that for tomorrow to tell. He stacks his drawings under the bed, on top of a summer's worth of drawings; he works on them sometimes in the afternoons, or cuts them up for collage; sometimes he just looks at them endlessly without deciding anything. There's no hurry. It's August, high tide, high season. The intense white light of July has lengthened and turned a golden color. Time slows a little, loose silk with light running through its folds, slack water, a ripple of grasses. It's late summer, rich and ripe, and every drop of it is gold.

TWENTY-THREE

❧

At Leisure

Water keeps what the sun gives it all day. Full jugs set by the rose bush wait through morning. By noon there's hot water for bathing. We strip off our suits and soap up in the high grass, pouring the water over ourselves in warm, trickling streams, washing through our salt-stuck hair, across arms, belly, breasts, and rounds of buttocks, the water running down our legs and over our feet, back into the sand, sloughing between the packed, slick grains, scouring salt and brine and suntan oil and sweat and sand and minute flakes of kelp from our skin. The white places our clothes covered seem doubly naked now. Inevitably, several times a week, the sightseeing plane will catch us standing there, wet and gleaming in our skins, with suds foaming our hair, and will circle over low, a reliable guffaw for the tourists who gape and go off, but though we shake our fists in the air and shout back at them, nothing can touch us. We're the savages of three miles from town, brazen, unvisited by missionaries. Children of the sun, we worship water—the vast salty ocean licking us clean, and the deep, single, sweet well-hole whose spring we prime and pump and carry and hoard in jugs and covered buckets, that is the single source of our life here.

When it came out of the ground, spurted from the steel lip of the pump, Bert's brown arm flexing to work the lever, then mine in turn, it was cold. Cold of a thousand years underground, rock caves with no sun, the first spring trapped in the ground forever flowing. It kept that memory, changing slowly all day as the light moved across the stone. Cold water touches us deep inside, fills our cells with a mineral light, and leaves a taste of iron in the mouth. We bring the fresh water with us, uphill. Heavy and still in the pail, its weight pulls our arms down. Covered in shadows, we hide it; it remembers what it is until dark.

Entering the board room, we blink in shadow, set the pails in the far corner under the stove, and cover them with tin plates to keep out the dust. I lean over to tug a comb through my wet hair; fat drops of water splat on the boards and disappear, soaking into the wood. Pulling my cotton robe loose around me, I feel the pleasures of my body, clean and sound, the long bones, and hard soles of my feet, the sweet brown flesh with its rising hunger. I will live and be strong forever.

Bert goes to hang the towels and swimsuits on the line, while I assess our options regarding lunch. Most days anything will do—soup from a can, or noodles in broth, something warm and quick—always crackers with peanut butter if nothing else comes to hand, maybe with olives on the side. One week we ate vienna sausages with hot mustard over and over; for another spell it was sweet peppers on toast. Today we'll stretch the remains of last night's chowder with a can of creamed corn and the last of the good bread, a little hard now, but good for dipping. We eat quietly with full attention, piling our plates high, and move slowly away from the table as we finish.

Clearing up, I steal a last bite from the side of the plate, swab my bread crust in the bowl. As we stack the dishes, shaking crumbs for the birds out the door, I feel at my back the growing lure of red plush covers stretched smooth across the bunks. I think I might lie down for just a minute, sinking on to the mattress, stretch out long and easy . . . Then I'm being scooted toward the edge as Bert climbs in after me, taking all the space so I have to press back against him or be flattened against the wall. It is, he reminds me, his bed. Our two bodies mold into a space meant for one. Staring up at the underside of the top bunk, tracing its maze of coils and knots and interlocking wires, I feel perplexed, unable to follow the pattern. I close my eyes. Everything is quiet, my head on his chest, his heart beating against my ear, our soft breaths rising and falling, familiar rhythm. Rub my back. Yes. The world stops. Endless time and we're in it, smack in the middle. One-thirty, two o'clock.

We lie together in the bunk and the sun glares on the windows, so far away. The room is dim, green in cave-light, our skin is cool and smooth; my fingers find their way up and down his chest, the soft curling hairs, up his neck, touching lazy, and his hand begins stroking me in slow long waves, a soothing motion accelerating with subversive intent. His hand snakes inside my robe and pulls to loosen the knot. He runs his open palm up my body and the fine hairs on my thighs and flanks drag against the grain, a friction that makes me shiver a little, raising my flesh in little bumps; he is leaning over me, supporting himself on one arm and with the other stroking gently, insistent, waking up every nerve ending and then I am pulling him closer and all the alive nerves in my skin are touching his skin, our bodies meeting along their whole lengths: leg, belly, forearm, breast. I move against him to feel his weight pressing down. Where touch goes blood follows, flows toward the feeling spot and floods it with sensation. A kiss drinking the body of the other: how many nerve endings in a tongue, tasting, licking, taking the breath—this is play, so easy, and then it shifts, every time it shifts, turns perilous and meaningful; our hearts race, breaths quicken, we open and swell and grip one another hard, fasten ourselves. Beneath the quiet face of desire lies starkest need; grown men and women will beg: don't stop, don't stop, don't stop . . . or even pray, oh God. And then lie breathing softly, not a space between their two bodies.

Meanwhile time passed and we served nothing and no one and the world went on without us. We entered, separately and together, a dedicated space, giving the world the slip, to join our bodies and breath. For nothing, for just the way it feels. This freedom, this thoroughly private zone of pleasure, threatens the order of nations: every society tries to contain it, wanting to know what, where, and with whom. Refusing to account to church or state, desire presses up—we find countless ways to elude jurisdiction.

When I was younger I used to count the times I'd "done it." Then I lost track. Maybe two hundred—three?—times a year? In a lifetime, what? More than ten thousand? What is the national average—does anybody keep records of these things? Yet we do it over and over; nearly everybody does, everybody more or less the same, the same repertoire of nerves and membranes. And for nothing. For pleasure. And because we do the world goes on and there are people in the world to do it, the whole world losing count, not numbering its own delight.

I lie here growing drowsy, warm, thinking this, imagining, for every person on earth, at least one instance when two someones let go of time and turned aside into their private space, thinking nothing of the world. The sweetness of that which is done for nothing, in the fullness of summer, in the late afternoon. I fall asleep with the sun on the windows, thinking this, satisfied as if something had been accomplished after all.

TWENTY-FOUR

&

Sitting Down to Supper

The afternoon grows late, and I begin to think of supper. There will be no surprises. Everything must be carried here on our backs, saved and afforded space on the narrow shelf over the west window or stuffed inside the small, ancient camp refrigerator, if it is working this week. There is what there is—everything visible at a glance, no surprises or last minute change of menu. We eat very well.

Today the larder is low—it's time for a trip to the dreaded A&P. Poorly stocked and overpriced, with narrow aisles, the summer crowds contending with increasingly hostile locals, all the employees fed up by July, the A&P is a dose of an alternate reality we try to deny from our privileged position two miles out of town.

Four o'clock: rice rattles in the bottom of the jar and other ready ingredients seem to consist of salt. Three days of heat have defeated the powers of the little fridge and yesterday we finished off wilting lettuce, brown-spotted pears, and a precious square of cheddar edged with mold. As ever when in doubt I set beans to boil, and slowly, around this homely nucleus, a meal begins to constellate, drawing bits and pieces to itself, and ordering each in relation to some slowly revealed whole. My friend Patricia Greene instructed me in the Spanish way to "punish the beans" —quicker than soaking, with the same effect. You boil them fast and hard for ten minutes and then plunge them into cold water, then simmer again. This weakens their internal structure, and apparently so confuses them that they just fall apart, entirely compromised, their self-image shot straight to hell.

Five o'clock, and the beans are cooking, dissolving into a broth helped along by a half teaspoon of olive oil coaxed from the seeming-empty bottle, some garlic and pepper. Rice steams secretly under its lid and the smell of what is becoming food lifts into the air, gathering strength in the shadows. Perhaps steam permeates the walls and releases old odors of meals—a memory held inside the wood, mixtures of spices and fat—or is this really grown so rich, just beans with oil, garlic and pepper, the actual faint smell of rice cooking?

I have a carrot and an onion. I'm chopping the onion three times—giving small chunks to the brown, softening beans, and hoarding raw slivers to sprinkle over them later, and I am shaving off translucent half circles to scorch in a hot skillet with the carrot. Liquor of onion is on my hands, sweet and pungent, leaching into the cutting board, shining on the knife blade. Each new surface releases flavors and essential juices. The fat, aging carrot turns to strips of gold, curling slightly at the ends as the knife finds surfaces within surfaces, exposing layer after layer, grain within grain, to release, from this compressed, dark root, mounds of gleaming orange shards. At the last minute they will tumble into the hot frying pan, along with crescents of onion, and, quickly stirred in hot oil, pile onto the sticky plain mound of rice. We will sit side by side on the bench before the window, substantial with our meal, its pleasures plain and full, eat everything, drink cool water from a cup, and wish for no more.

Other nights we sit down with friends who arrive late, bearing news and bottles of wine, who come out for the beach and stay for supper. They bring us treats from town: newspapers and peaches, cold beers, fresh gossip. Ken and Harriet showed up three days ago, by surprise of course; every visit in the dunes is a surprise.

They brought fish and wine, and were followed, within the half hour, by our friend Roger, who surprised us all even further by bringing nothing. The fish—a fine slab of cod—was firm, dense and white; it flaked off in layers when it was well cooked, and I fried up potatoes in the big cast-iron pan. We cooled the wine in a bucket of pump water and drank from little cups, and ate and talked, sitting out on the hill under the weathervane. The taste of fish on my tongue, sweet, with a spray of lemon, and our friends' names on our lips—we took the last half loaf of bread, cut off the stale crusts and dipped it into the buttery sauce and ate until the wind came up, driving sand into our plates, and then we moved inside. Five of us disposed ourselves around the cabin, two on the bench, backs to the table, plates on their laps, one on the bottom bunk, two of us cross-legged on the floor. I served seconds from the corner by the stove, and we argued loudly over someone we all knew in town, waving our forks in the air, our faces flushed with the day's sun. Afterwards we piled up the plates and went out to watch the sunset from the hill. The dunes were turning deep gold as the sun rolled down the side of the earth. We sat with our legs drawn up to our chests as the great ball lowered and flattened itself along the horizon, squeezing out light, turning the clouds pink and blue.

"Look at the grass," Bert said suddenly, pointing down the hill, and at that instant the grasses turned silver along their entire lengths, a platinum overexposure, dancing like photographic ghosts, as the long rays of sun slid up the hill, lighting them from beneath. Spears of translucent color bands raced along each stem and blade—red and purple and yellowish green glinting as the sun went down in a big red lump, melting into hill and water. Moments later it sent up a dusky afterglow, thinning to streaks of pink, and a pulsing bank of sullen embers.

Ken poured out the last of the wine, and we sat and waited for the second sunset that always comes just when you think the sunset is over, when it returns and stretches along the horizon, diffuse and somber, and deeper than any color you have seen there before.

This second sunset, this echo of sunset, spread around the horizon, growing darker, and then the first stars began to appear. We turned the wine bottle upside down in the sand and it hung there glinting, a jade object, waist-deep in shadow, floating clouds in its giant fish-eye, until it too went dark like the end of a prophecy.

And before anyone was ready they had to leave to find their way home across the dunes while there was still some light. Bert and I watched from the hill until they were out of sight; then we went inside and lit the lamps and heated water and carefully washed and dried the plates and the glasses and the silver, the big fry pan and the smaller one with bits of fish burned into its center.

This is a story Hazel told me:

One evening almost fifty years ago, Jack and Wally Tworkov walked out to Thalassa to eat supper with Hazel. The sun was glinting off the grass spears and smearing the windows gold as they came over the rise. Inside, they could hear Hazel moving about—from shelf to stove, water jug to dish rack—busy with preparations. Coming around the side of the shack, they passed the west window and peeked in: the room was filled with rainbows! Hazel was moving in colored bands of light that danced on the glasses, and glinted and leaped at the walls. Jack and Wally came inside, exclaiming, and when she turned to look the rainbows danced faster, and they were thrown from the glass beads she was wearing with her summer dress that night. It was only a brief time that the sun came in the windows at just such an angle to turn glass beads into prisms, and for a little while they all sat together, talking as supper cooked, and red and green and blue bursts of light rose and fell with her movements, fading slowly as the sun went down behind the west window and all the colors died.

Stories of summer endure. We all sat together one winter night looking at pictures. Hazel recalled an evening sixty-five years before, when she sat on the town beach while the moon rose, and listened to laughter floating from high windows, coming from a party at Eugene O'Neill's. She was sixteen and her mother would not allow her to attend the wild "carousels" of the writer and his friends, but she was a little wild too, and pretty, and full of wanting, and the sounds of that party filled her with a longing two-thirds of a century has not taken from her voice as she tells it, turning pages of an album with hands that tremble. They are all dead now, she said. They had many parties, and in later years she would go, but that is the only one she really remembers.

They talked of later summers, when the artists came and galleries began to open along Commercial Street. One summer everyone's marriage broke up. Jack tried to remember whether he had known Hazel then. "I had a red beard," he said, and she nodded doubtfully. They recalled a woman they both knew, the summer temptress of that year. She drove all the men crazy, a mysterious, sylph-like creature, older than the rest of them, with a rich husband back in Philadelphia. What was her name? No one remembers. "I was a little in love with her myself," Jack confessed. "What kind of expression is that, a little in love?" Wally demanded to know.

We sat listening to the old people talk. Someone should remember all this, the bits of history, the stories we're sure to get wrong when we try to tell them again. But I am too moved to take them as history, to try to store them up. I think of my own memories of summer, of summer turning into the past, and of time passing. It's winter and the wind huffs and coughs in the chimney and as we sit there I can feel this evening already going away, hear the voices of the old people and I can feel us losing them, and going after, not able to follow.

Fifty or sixty years later, what is it to have been "a little in love" with someone you can't quite remember, someone quite possibly dead for years? A memory of forbidden parties, of being too young and seeing a life half glimpsed just beyond you. All of it coming toward you then, the world coalescing its energies to flower in you, intense and personal and full of pent-up longings? How strange that we were ever too young, that we have seemed for so long to be just approaching the absolute moment, and then years have passed, summers, and laughter from open windows, and the slow fading radiance of the evenings. Someone should re-member all this, we should begin remembering now, how slow the summer can be, how many layers there are to pleasure, the fullness of it, how much remains when even the names are gone.

We sit down to supper later now, at our table under the window. Our hunger tamed, we take our time. In Euphoria there is time to rest, to prop our arms on the table as we eat and gaze out the win-dow down the dune and across the water. Sometimes Bert tunes in a baseball game on the radio; we feel a distant companionship with the calm, statistics-remembering voices that arrive from over the sea, blown east from the mainland. Boston, Maine, New Bed-ford. Dark makes the shack cozy, the room gathering shadows into itself. Nothing more could be wanted, except perhaps a square of chocolate to nibble with coffee, but we don't have that, and besides the coffee tin is empty, there isn't any milk, and we really will need to go to the damned A&P. It doesn't matter. Soon the sun will set. The horseback riders are moving along the beach. We sit down to supper at our table made of salvaged boards, with our menu of what is, and are grateful.

TWENTY-FIVE

Night Lights

Satellites in the sky, at first mistaken for stars, that night we stayed awake to watch the moon's eclipse. Bert is there and our friend Susan, who is a sculptor. They are talking straight up into the sky and staring at the full white moon, just beginning to be covered over as our planet moves its shadow across the surface. Warmth is rising up from the earth, around them and through them; their voices hover in the space warmed by breath. Susan is describing a way of tying branches together with vines, inventing sculptures in thin air. Their lines, frozen in the cutting, still give an illusion of motion. The problem is how to make them stand up. It's not geometry, she says, her voice high and quick with speculation, but it's not nature either. I come out, balancing mugs of coffee, and sit down beside them. They are talking about the branches and then the conversation turns to a friend who has just broken another promise. That's just how he is, we finally agree; you can't take it personally. Expectation has crashed up and cracked its head against this person's ways so many times that just being able to see a pattern in it is reassuring. It becomes a story, a tale that can be told over and over. As we speak, our words are thrown up against the sky and hang there in a grid. They hesitate a moment, glittering, and then disperse into the air.

The eclipse began after midnight, a simple darkening of the moon's phases in fast time. Waiting for it to begin, we lit the shack with every lamp we could find—eight oil lamps flared in the dark, sending flickering shadows up the walls. The place looked like a Western saloon from outside, a bright raw hole in the night, full of jazzed-up talk and laughter risen unnaturally loud. We drank some vodka, but it made us sleepy so I put on coffee. We tried to be interested in scrabble, and then gin rummy. Can you play poker with three? I don't know, how do you play poker? By eleven-thirty everything was going silent. The only thing for it then was to blow out the lamps and go out in the warm night, to walk down to the beach, the grasses bright in the moonlight and the tops of the waves glinting silver as the tide pitched them up the beach. The water shimmered and gleamed where the light hit it, but under the surface the ocean was dark and wild, alive with riptides, currents, fish running up the coast. We stood and watched the lights out at sea, where a few ships were passing, and some anchored far out, with lanterns hung on their masts. Highland Light swept its beam across the Truro hills, and a change of wind brought voices from a boat. "Come forward," a man's voice said clearly, and whatever reply there was blew away toward High Head as they sailed on south.

As the moon darkened, the stars started to come out, faint at first, then growing brighter. We lay on a sleeping bag spread open on the sand, and heard the little toads hopping about beside us in the grass. Lying there, gazing up, we talked easily of anything that came to our minds, our voices warm and matter-of-fact, our breaths crossing in the dark.

Is that a satellite? It has such a strange path it must be—or maybe a UFO! People tell of sightings on the Cape, seem to remember abduction in dream. It seems possible, anything's possible, what do we know? Now the moon was nearly dark and we could see all the stars and so much else glittering above us: satellites and garbage from spaceships, cosmic junk, occasional flaring meteors, and low, irregular paths of airplanes beginning their journeys out over the black ocean. And were there cosmonauts still circling up there in the lost, unrecovered satellites? I remembered horror stories of the sixties, desperate tales of transmissions picked up from Mexico, spacemen, always Russians in our stories, pleading to be brought down, then losing radio contact and floating off in space forever. But we are spacemen too.

We spoke to one another in resonant, calm voices. Meanwhile I was looking at the sky and gradually, abetted by a certain detached concentration, I was able to feel myself turning over, to make it so the sky was floating below me and I was sailing, with the planet pasted to my back far above it. The stars were revolving as usual from east to west, around the North Pole. Now I looked down at the stars. I had come out for the eclipse but it was the stars I watched, growing brighter as the moon dimmed. We rush, falling, into those distant lights, the stars where we can never, ever go. Most of them are further away each time we look, accelerating into the distance and someday there will be no starlight at all. No one will lie here and search the sky—what we call "here" will have disappeared. I felt serene as if we'd lived long ago, as if our life here were a warm, affectionate memory.

Watching the stars, these thoughts descend calmly. You shift focus and forget for a while to identify with the small person drawing breath after breath in the shelter of a sand bank, lying on a sleeping bag with pictures of cowboys on it. Instead you become the mind of that person, limitless and cold, sailing out above the earth.

Bert had been studying the constellations all summer and he began to point them out as they appeared. "Over there, that's Sagittarius, that's mine," he said. I never had much interest in those myths—I knew these points of light had no relation to one another in deep space; their patterns described, as I thought, nothing real, distorting the three-dimensional universe to a false theatrical backdrop. Patiently he would trace Draco, Ursa Minor,

Perseus, the long "W" of Cassiopeia, but nothing about these shapes was obvious to me; only the Big Dipper really looked like what it was supposed to be. Stories of kings and gods, anyway, what could they mean?

But lying there like that, gazing long into the sky, for moments I could see the sky flatten out and imagine figures scrawled across the black. Patterns created by our viewpoint, confirming us. That we have a viewpoint, that we are in fact here in this place and time, to see the shining lights as they appear to us.

The astrological signs, and their constellations, come to us from the Chaldeans. Their scrutiny of the heavens was long and thoughtful, revealing nothing less than a divine order. How must it have been to think like a Chaldean, to scan the sky for prophecy, predicting eclipses of the sun and moon, to calculate, for the first time in human existence, the length of a year? They managed wonderfully accurate observations, patiently watching, night after night, in the clear desert sky, a whole priesthood of skywatchers, seeing a fixed universe above a central earth. The people of Nebuchadnezzar II, who rebuilt Babylon and destroyed the temple of Jerusalem, the priests who measured the year and the cycles of the moon, could, with all their learning, have counted forward to this very night, this eclipse where we lie watching the ancient moon go dark again. It was all foreseen, changeless, part of the story they told; and at last only the stories matter.

We no longer believe those stories, and the stars seem farther away from us than ever. No longer do we look to the sky for prophecy or observe festivals in accordance with the rising of certain stars. Who knows the summer constellations and the winter constellations and follows their changes through the seasons? We can't believe that gods reside in that visible heaven, that Orion hunts in the night, or see the Centaur draw his bow. Those old shapes have meaning only when we think of navigating, using them to gauge movement and direction if we were lost without instruments—but who among us gets lost anymore, even venturing so far off the path that the sky can open for us?

The view from the front of Euphoria tonight is perhaps three hundred trillion miles. Looking up, our gaze penetrates this atmosphere, this solar system and galaxy, to look beyond its own lifetime and be met by arriving light. A typical distance between stars is five light years, or about thirty trillion miles. Traveling by jet I could reach the nearest star in about six million years.

On a clear night we may see two thousand stars. The Milky Way spreads over us, the "path of ghosts" in Norse mythology, one hundred thousand light years across, its tail flared out from the engulfing center, swirling like water down a drain. Writhing in slow time, this shining trail appears to be going out, perhaps being pulled into a black hole. The stars we see, which may or may not still exist, give us the wrong impression. The universe is essentially empty—and still expanding. Atoms are mostly empty space, protons and neutrons spinning in clouds of little electrons, held together by invisible forces. The nucleus is only one quadrillionth of the atom's volume. If you enlarge the nucleus to the size of a bowling ball, the atom would be twenty miles across. My body is a void, and an "empty quarter" of the cosmos has recently been found—a void, measuring thirty septillion cubic light years. A three and twenty-five zeros, written like this: 30,000,000,000, 000,000,000,000,000, a place with no forms or light or mass, only cold dark matter.

But we're here. Briefly, in the path of ancient light, in an empty universe, there are places of presence and we are one of these. I look at the sky; an ant crawls up my leg. I hear the voices of the others near me, warmth and motion as we lie here, falling out of orbit, racing toward the center of the Virgo supercluster, sixty million light years away.

When Nebuchadnezzar captured Jerusalem in 587 BC, his army broke the bronze pillars of the temple and scattered the people abroad, so they became a people not of a place but of a law and a book; people held to this day by the story they kept. Then there was Nebuchadnezzar himself, maddened by prophecy, on his hands and knees in the fields, eating grass.

It is important what story you choose. The new ones we tell ourselves, about light years, quasars, quarks and cold matter, are stories of vast distances and unimaginable, dematerializing reality. These stories amaze and chasten, but also alienate us. The stars now remind us of our powerlessness and insignificance, our isolation, signaling the end of our world and time.

We need to imagine the story further, to refigure it without denying what we know. We need a new story about the stars. Though the boldness of numbers makes us catch our breath and marvel, and the vast calculations which dismiss the material world titillate our minds, we humans cannot live with utter alienation. The story needs to draw us closer, to bring the universe once more into us through our bodies and felt rhythms.

The story might again be one of navigation. Sailors crossing an uncharted sea to new worlds were no more lost than we feel when we imagine the galaxies flying apart. Can we steer by these stars still—can we use them, so far out there ahead of us, can we follow the stars out of time as we are flung toward Virgo, and beyond?

The moon, however, is ours. We have touched her, and brought back rocks from her surface, her very body. We have photographs of earth rising over the moon's horizon. Those voyages to the moon are circular; it would be counted disaster were they not to return, whereas star journeys are sent outward, drifting endlessly into the dark.

Intimately as we have touched her, she touches us. Her tides draw up and back on this narrow strip of sand—we are flooded and constricted, then released—water converging and dispelled. These tides are in our blood. We see her face change in the sky from day to day; we wax and wane. Corn Moon, Pink Moon, Hunter's Moon, these designations corresponding to earthly seasons still hold our imaginations. On a full moon, an electric energy prevails on the land; we lie awake, thrilled by a ghostly light. It's not the brightness alone that keeps us awake—I could turn my face to the wall—but her wakeful presence charging the world, a spirit shining out of the deep backdrop of night, holding the black sky at her shoulder.

At the moment of full eclipse, when the last sliver of moon, a chip of light, a clipped fingernail, a slit in black cloth barely present in the deep black sky, was covered up, another moon appeared. This moon, in the exact place of the old white one, was a dark and fiery red, a coal of a moon glowering above us. It changed all at once from a nothing of passive, dissolving light, into an angry ghost whose fierce light rang against the sky, a red disc one-sixth the size of the world, looming near and round and personal, not to be mastered. Set against the sun, we cast our big shadow across the moon, and the emptied sky protested.

This lasted only moments and then the shadow moved onward, uncovering the moon from the other side. The first glint of cool light put out the fire. The moon began to grow again, and the stars blinked out. By two in the morning there was a quarter moon with light clouds blowing across it. Bert and Susan went inside to sleep, and I lay on the sand, still traveling.

I woke at dawn, stiff and cold, a quilt over my shoulders, the sleeping bag bunched up beneath me. The full moon hung over the southwest dune, opaque and yellow, the eastern sky greying with light. As the sun approached the horizon, it took all color for its own, bleaching the moon to shell-white, then melting it like ice. I shook myself and got up, walked across the yellow sand and up the steps into the shadowed dawn of Euphoria. Susan was in my bunk and Bert lay sprawled across his, so I rolled out a mat and lay down on the floor to sleep.

TWENTY-SIX

❧

Another Fish Story

Walking toward Race Point last night after supper, down where the sandbar is uncovered at low tide, Bert and I ran into a fishing party out from town. Bluefish were running alongshore, setting off a great rush of excitement on the beach, a lot of shouting, and movement in every direction. We stopped to watch. A deep-tanned man with strong-muscled arms and a big voice played the expert; he walked calmly backward, pulling his fish into shallow water, keeping the rod bent and the line tight as he shouted out instructions to his friends. A pot-bellied man wearing a t-shirt which proclaimed "I Am A Wild And Crazy Guy" lost three in a row, pulling up too sharply, not taking time to play the line. Finally, he landed one and stomped back up the beach in a black humor. Their wives were there with them, taking pictures of the fish, of the fishermen, of each other, and the big blues arched and flapped on the sand, flashing sharp, pointed teeth, and the men laughed and pulled the hooks out of their mouths with pliers, moving quickly, in a hurry for more.

Then everyone was catching them. A motorboat pulled in close to shore and a van stopped in its tracks and three men got out and waded out on the sandbar to cast. Everyone was catching the strong, blue-green fish that jerked the line, bent poles almost in half, that flashed out of the water, breaking, and were hauled up on shore. It was exciting, gorgeous with the scent of slaughter, the bodies coming in so fast, long and lovely. Blue-green scales with silver underneath turned dull as the life went out of them, no light in the eyes. A dune tour, and then another, stopped to let their riders out. Men in Bermuda shorts took pictures of other men's catch, pictures of fish in the air, fish on the beach, and we stood among the crowd, feeling their excitement sparking up like drops of water shaken in the air. Then we walked on.

"Why don't we ever go fishing?" I wondered, not remembering that we don't have equipment, or know how.

"You fish, I'll take your picture," Bert offered, framing me with his hands and crouching down. I posed, hand on hip, chest thrust forward, pouting. "Beautiful, baby, keep it coming!"

Further down the beach we could still see the fishermen, their figures small in the distance, moving jerkily like marionettes. We turned, following the curve and sweep of the shoreline away from them until we could see nothing. By the time we came back the fish, the fishermen, the boats, and the onlookers were all gone and the beach was empty again. Blues are like that; they go by all at once in a hurry, and you just have to be there when they are.

This stretch along Race Point is known as one of the best surf-casting beaches on the east coast, and is a long-standing source of controversy. Thousands of people come from all over New England to fish here every summer: amateurs and sportsmen and commercial fishermen. But lately the Park Service has taken to closing parts of the beach to off-road vehicles for interims, in an attempt to protect endangered terns and piping plovers, which nest here. Every year we suffer the same outcries in the local newspaper, as fishermen argue with the rangers and local conservationists over beach access. The idea that a handful of tern or plover chicks can close down a strip of prime summer beach for weeks doesn't make sense to those who worship the sacred mystery of the internal combustion engine. The idea of running down tern chicks in the wheel tracks doesn't sit right with the other side, so things get self-righteous on both ends. Eventually the beach-buggy contingent is portraying itself as composed of itinerant hunter-gatherers and subsistence fishermen (in $35,000 fully equipped micro-vans) while the other side is evoking Thoreau and Gandhi and claiming to faint at the sound of a motor. None of which has much to do with the terns, the plovers, or any sensible accommodation thereof.

Historically this beach has been a place of industry and sustenance, not a preserve in any sense we might mean today. It's been a garbage dump and a morgue too, you might as well argue; until the turn of the century it was common practice for townspeople to throw their garbage—everything from vegetable peels to cast iron washtubs—right into the harbor. But the men who fished and gathered firewood on the beach in those days went on foot, and this limited their impact. It's good to see the beach used instead of only visited, to renew the commerce between lives that runs so deep in the imagination of this place. I'm of two or three minds here—I can't take the arguments for driving on the beach seriously, and I deplore many of the assumptions that drive them. But I like the fishermen.

Along the coast up in New Hampshire, bluefish have been biting swimmers. Five people were treated at a state beach after bluefish bit their feet; we read about it in the paper. The bathers suffered cuts on the soles of their feet and puncture wounds on their insteps and ankles. It was a hot day, and the blues had some mackerel cornered in a cove where people were swimming. A heavy surf had churned white water into a froth, and a whole mob of blues went charging through, slashing left and right, mistaking flutter kicks for fins and feet for dinner.

Fish bites man. The papers must have been elated, but it's not hard to believe when you're talking about blues. Anyone who has seen bluefish in a feeding frenzy can attest to this creature's appalling proclivities. Fast, voracious, vicious, a school of blues will charge full speed into a school of smaller fish, striking at anything that moves. The arrival of a crowd of bluefish on the grounds must send the same bolt of panic through the sober citizens of the deep that the approach of Viking ships produced in the matrons of seaside villages eight hundred years ago. We saw a kill last summer down toward Phil Malicoat's shack, just five or six yards off shore. It was the terns we saw first, from a distance, wheeling and dive-bombing over the spray, frantically zigzagging the air. It looked like the surface of the water was exploding, blue waves detonating into white, as if the terns' dives were scattering the surface. When we got closer we saw the water thick with sand eels, flipping and thrashing in a charge to get away from the bluefish who were chasing them in toward shore. The sand eels pressed forward in confusion, one on another, sometimes leaping straight out of the water as if evolution could speed up in an instant to give them wings. The waves glistened with thousands of finger-length silver bodies as they were driven up the beach. The beach itself squirmed with stranded sand eels. Only a few feet offshore, the water boiled with bluefish, their torpedo bodies rising and plunging, as terns and then gulls wheeled overhead, screaming, dipping down to pick up bits of torn flesh that floated in the water. The birds were careful not to dive completely under the water for fear the blues would eat them too.

Like many such attacks, this one simply ended when the bluefish abandoned the chase, leaving behind a rouge-tinted water, floating shreds of scales and flesh, and seagulls massed along shore feasting on the beached remains.

A bluefish can weigh up to thirty pounds, though the ones I've seen have been not much over ten. They are long, stout fish, with blue-green scales, shading to silver on the belly, a pointed snout, and a big mouth full of sharp teeth that can cut through nets, bite through a line, or take a man's finger down to the bone. They like riptides and clashing currents, are creatures of chaos, and will strike at anything that moves. All appetite and rage for destruction, they chew up much more than they can consume, and bite off somewhat more than that; they will even eat and then regurgitate in order to gorge themselves again. Dark and fatty, their flesh has the wild taste of the sea in it, slightly sweet, with a penetrating odor. The meat is dark and comes away in ragged strips, a heavy, sustaining dish that stands up well to strong drink. Walt Whitman always maintained a particular fondness for a bluefish dinner, savoring the hearty flavor of the fish. Fishermen say you can tell when a school is nearby by an oily slick on the water, and a faint smell of cut watermelon, or some say cucumber, whereas striped bass, for instance, are said to smell like thyme.

If bluefish are the brutes, the surf's barbarians, the striped bass is the glamour fish of these waters, particular, even sensitive, as the bluefish most definitely is not. Their long, compressed bodies have a particular elegance as they wind along the coast, following baffling, indiscernible patterns. They appear flashing in the surf, a metallic sheen along their sides, a hint of gold, and dark olive green, two fins on their backs pointing upward. Where bluefish come in mobs, their schools sometimes covering several acres, full-grown stripers tend to be solitary, or to travel in pairs, hugging the shore between the tide levels, where they find crabs, squid, small fish and razor clams. Toothless, they have to swallow their dinner whole—this makes them think twice before striking and earns them a reputation for being finicky, or even intelligent. They are said to like "live water," the turbulent, oxygen-rich shallows, but are extremely disturbed by surf. Elusive and unpredictable, loners in the classical sense, they are a highly prized catch. Their flesh has a delicacy, and an elegant texture, all firm and white, that the restaurant crowd goes crazy for. A big one can bring good money, if you can bear to part with it.

There is a certain mystique about the striped bass. They are the fisherman's enigma, the muse of these cold waters. Stripers seem to come by magic, to an individual call, prompting superstitious thinking. Stripers drive fishermen crazy—they stay up all night for weeks casting for them, an affliction known as "striper fever" and recognized as grounds for divorce in many households. People tend to have stories about stripers they have caught, remembering them for years, whereas a bluefish is just dinner.

Bert and I turned homeward under a soft grey, luminous sky, picking up feathers and sticks, walking in the jeep tracks. I found a quarter and a fish bone. Neither any good to me here. The bone shone white and clean, very hard, and sharp at one end, like something useful, and the quarter glinted darkly in my hand. Why not a doubloon, or pieces of eight? Why not a bottle of pirate's rum, coughed up from the belly of a whale? What might not rise out of these dark, shining waters, what unimagined treasure might the tide leave behind when it slides down the beach? I always think I'm going to find just one diamond necklace: there must be hundreds out there.

Bert stopped me as I stood staring at the sand, and pointed out over the water. In the soft twilight, two harbor seals were swimming on the shoals. Playmates, or a pair, their cat whiskers twitching with curiosity, they seemed to be following us, diving and coming up as we walked along, gazing back toward the land with intelligent dark eyes. One dark head would pop up in the waves, big eyes staring wetly across the distance, then it would dive and swim along the beach, coming up after a half minute or so. One then the other. Soft brown shadows, they roam the shoreline, pretty creatures, fish-eaters, with the coarse hair on their cigar-shaped bodies, their sleek, glossy heads. The seals rose and dove, playing in the twilight surf like ghosts, spirits with kind eyes, at home there, peaceful, with nowhere they had to go. A couple of fishing boats riding low in the water steered back around Race Point past Wood End. The water was calm and warm, pressing forward and curling back. Up ahead some fishermen were setting up for the night, their squat, navy blue van catching the sun's last rays, darkly flaring along its side.

The eyes of fish, like the eyes of birds, return no gaze. They take in light, respond to movement, but do not meet you. Theirs is a long stare, beyond particulars; they swim in global currents, go where we can't follow. We don't know much about fish, where they come from, where they go, even how long they live. To see them you have to train your eyes to look through the surface glare, where the water refracts light, to look past the reflections of the sky held there, down through light glancing inside the water. The living fish is a mystery, glimpsed for a single moment when it is hauled up into the air, struggling, caught by the hunger that hooks us all. We eat, while we live, from the banquet of the living, our food fresh with life juices. This is the fish story, how life lives on life, everything nourishing that current.

There are several brands of wildness in the world, elusive or savage, or modest and patient, various ways of living outside the world's understanding and control. It is not necessary to choose among them. The fish may come in a rush, breaking the water, maddening the waves, straining furiously at the line, and you may pull in one after another, working yourself into a frenzy as they fight you. Or one fish may come as a single possibility out of the wide dark waves where it threads its way along shore; it may strike, or slip by without your noticing. Or maybe you will pull it in and, as in the old story, it will grant you three wishes.

TWENTY-SEVEN

❧

A Late Walk

We've been to town twice this week, a social whirl for us, first to a birthday party, and then to a friend's gallery opening. When we walk back at night, the dunes are a new mystery. If there is any moon, or even bright starlight, the sand glows dimly and we walk at ease across this wide, unworldly world, feeling sure of our way, and tolerant of every sound and movement. A dry smell rises as our feet scuff the sand; toads hop in the grass, and the dry bogs give off a stench both rich and rank. To stroll through a wide, shadowed landscape, over cool white sands, among the secret leaves of the cranberry growing next to the ground, is a vast and peaceful pleasure, though we do tend to scare the deer. We pass through woods and over the big bald dune, then down across the moors, quietly awake with poverty grass, scrub pines and sheep laurel. Then we cross the jeep trail where the old oak stands bent double with salt winds, its grey leaves sweeping the sand. Dessicate and twisted, bent ever more radically downward, flat at the crown, it gives an impression of constant pain. Past the crossroads the trail begins to climb and cuts through a dune into the blow-out where the rusted metal hulks sit gathering shadow. We climb the path, cut across to the little footpath by the pump, then straight uphill to where Euphoria sits, dark and closed, the big padlock hanging from the latch, and all the windows shut tight.

We come up the path and look around for tracks, to see that no one has been here, that nothing has been disturbed. Returning to an isolated place at night, there is a quick current of fear, and then a feeling of comfort once we see that all is well.

Returning to Euphoria at night, turning the lock, pressing open the heavy door, I always feel a deep sense of privacy and possession. The inner dark is denser, blacker, than the dark that lies across the land. Inside, the air has not moved for hours, and in the gloom our things lie still, books and silverware, the breakfast dishes dry now, a hush all over the place. A house on the dunes— as if it were truly ours. Shack, shelter, hut, hull, or shell of boards, it is ours if anything is. No less borrowed than our bones, it holds our lives and we call it home, returning at night out of the wide dark world.

We go in and do not light the lamps, but sit on the steps, drinking cool water from coffee mugs, gazing across cloud-shadowed dunes, secure in our only life, where mice play in the grasss and the old moon is just rising. The house of boards rises at our backs. We sit there long, gazing and pondering, and then we go in to bed, passing from dark into dark.

On our second trip from town this week there was no moon and a thick haze covered the sky. The party had been loud and happy, and it was past midnight when our drowsy, exhilarated friends dropped us at the trailhead. We stepped away from the light and noise of the car, the radio and all our voices talking at once, back into the damp, overhanging trees. Our friends drove off and the highway lay quiet and black behind them. Bert flipped on the flashlight and we hoisted our packs loaded with clean laundry from the morning's errand, and turned our faces toward the path.

It was like stepping off the edge of the world, and for a moment I swam in panic while the woods reestablished its presence around us. Stepping forward on the path, I was suddenly very drunk. It hit me like a wave across the sandbar, knocking me sideways, dizzy and floating at once. Reeling, lifted, I was afraid to ask Bert if he felt the same thing for fear he did, and instead fell quietly in step beside him, following the spotlight of our single lantern along the floor of the woods.

We walked under the trees for some incalculable amount of time and finally came into the open. I expected it to be brighter, but there was only a faint sensation of inanimate presences pulling back, a release into a dense, watery darkness. There was no sky, and all I could see were our feet in a bald patch of light going forward again and again across the trackless sand. A foot would appear, shift, another come up from behind to replace it, and so on continually, a blue sneaker and a white one, each followed by its likeness. We walked, and after some time I began to realize that I not only had no idea of direction, but I could not assure myself that we were even moving. I had the unnerving sensation that we were walking in one spot, that we had always been walking, that we were nowhere at all. It seemed that time had stopped, that this walking nowhere went on forever. There were just our feet treading forward in a single beam of light, the untracked sand we stepped down on continually, and nothing before or behind. Finally, in a small, I hoped not very concerned-sounding voice, I asked Bert, "Where are we now?" and after a slight pause a very quiet answer came back: "I was hoping you knew."

We felt the ground under us rise and fall, going who-knows-where, too muddled to stop and reconsider, too dazed to properly panic. Briefly, the long slope of the big dune steadied us as we climbed, and we grasped at a sense of progress. But even this security was shattered as we gradually felt ourselves going up sideways, crablike, with no downhill anywhere in evidence and nothing like a trail or a footprint in sight. We put our feet down one after the other in a spot of light held flickering in Bert's hand and kept walking blindly through the world.

Drunkard's luck, the feel of the path, the wakening of senses we don't usually pay attention to, led us home that night in spite of ourselves. We did not find our way: we were led, not knowing the world. Had it been so dark and we been sober we might not have given into whatever sense guided us; we might have second guessed and blundered and gone off the path and wandered further afield. At least, this is what I believe. I know we reached Euphoria by abandoning effort, giving ourselves up in the most irrational way, and falling homeward. We found our beds, I think by sense of smell, as homing salmon do, as we swam home across the dark hills. Attaining the doorway, we crossed over and fell down together in the bottom bunk where we lay unmoving as the night air floated through the screens, and when the sun came shooting over the hill at six o'clock, it caught me in the eye and I rolled over once and Bert never moved at all.

The nights stay warm now straight through till dawn, but the days are getting shorter. The sun rises later every day, just a minute or two, you'd barely notice. A few minutes absorbed at each end, less than fifteen minutes lost in a week, hardly worth considering. Waking late to go stare at the cool pinpricks of stars, the sweep of Highland Light bearing across the hills, I see the whole Milky Way spread across the sky. Already Orion is hauling himself up over Highland Light, one shoulder out of the water, following me as I turn back to bed. It is August; we sleep through many sunrises now.

September

I will not forget you. See, I have carved you in the palm of my hand.

Isaiah 49:16

TWENTY-EIGHT

❧

The Star Flower

Bright air of September, red in the oak leaves, burnt orange in the fattening rosehips. Huckleberry blazes through piney undergrowth. We walked all afternoon in bright sun, across the open dunes, into oak and pine woods, through shadows and clearings. The leaves hung flamey and big on the trees where the path climbed steeply up from the pond. At the edge of the woods, the sand dunes opened, spilling across to the deep blue of the Atlantic, and a glimpse of Euphoria's slanting roof. We walked all afternoon together, taking the sun into our bodies, breathing salt and loam and leaf mold mixed with the spice of wintergreen crushed underfoot. Pine cones flared their scales, their seeds cast wide, and cluster flies hung in patches of bright air, dancing in ceaseless motion, never lighting or going away. Now the rain is on the roof, tapping against the walls, a small, slow rain that will last for hours. I turn in soft worn sheets, warm with my body's warmth, sand in their creases, and as I turn I am walking, climbing and circling back, gazing down the slope to the pond, then climbing up the hill where we rested in sunlight at the edge of the woods.

This is the best time of year for walking, these mid-September afternoons with their clear, transparent light. The air is cooler on the dunes now, their soft flanks rippling along the horizon where the sky lifts up, unfolding rafts of cumulus, and alto-stratus whips, with side seas of renaissance blue between. These days the sun is an animate, changing presence, played in layers and shafts of light, lighting up great clouds with bright white edges and swirling, seal-grey centers. The dunes shimmer, gold hills folding into green and brown troughs, a line of pines darkening the seam of a valley.

It is a familiar fiction that this season brings endings. This shows perhaps our prejudice, in a still-new culture, for the seed-head over the root. We see the leaves' turning as a prefigurement of death, but it is simply a change, after all, a discarding that allows the trees to survive. The world is never any older in one season than another, or any closer to its beginning.

Yet September, in its own right, is hard to imagine: it seems so always on the verge of being something else, so not-quite-finished with what went before. September seems not entirely to be *here*— it is always earlier or later, leaning back into the last of summer or charging ahead into cold, and it is an act of will to focus it, to take each changing day for itself alone. Clarity demands a quick look round, a sharp eye for detail, and a refusal to extend the evidence by implication. It is a moral act to see September, to see what is and no more, to feel it around you and to let your mind rest there.

We took a long route today, beginning up behind Euphoria where we searched for beach plums but didn't find any. We continued back into the dunes, heading west, down into the hollow behind Phil Malicoat's shack, circling the bog where long reddish vines of wild cranberry trail over the sand. The berries are just beginning to ripen. Finches flitted in and out of the scrub brush, domestic, busy, making a little colony of this green valley.

Across the open dunes, we climbed up to the furthest rim where the woods hold their line against tons of encroaching sand. We scrambled down a sandbank and the trees closed in around us. The trail was dusted with pale, greyish sand filtered down from above; black earth showed underneath. Under the trees was a world of shadow and light between branches, layers of undergrowth, a complexity of lives. These woods are old, with well-worn paths and walls of green, filled with rich soil and marks of use. Asters blinked in shafts of light, catching the sun in their tips. A tang of pine resin filled the air; the leaves glinted and shook themselves over webs swollen and sagging with dew.

Bert walked ahead on the narrow path. His long, easy strides soon gathered speed and I let him outpace me, sensing his impatience for what lay ahead. He seemed eager and pleased with the rhythm of his walking, moving energetically forward. I lagged in my own time, looking left and right and up and down, mentally stepping off the path into the infinite distances between here and there.

There is the path the deer took when they flashed out of sight one evening last spring, the doe and her fawn together. The little one was curious and stopped to look back a minute. Their trail is hardly visible now, a mere trampling in the bush. Purple thistles sat high atop their stems, tightly bunched like the compound eyes of flies, and a fallen tree lay across a small clearing, its bark half-peeled away, moss growing furry and wet across its roots. Milkweed seeds blew toward me like great photos of atoms, listing side to side and slowly winding, making visible the currents of air that drove them. Fat bumblebees bumped against the asters, white and violet clusters springing up on weedy stalks. When I see the asters I know it is September. The last flowers of summer, they bloom just as other flowers are fading. Aster is Greek for "star," and though they take their name from the stiff radiating petals around their heads, they seem star-like also in coming out so late, to shine against a darkness of green. Their petals open bright and showy, but at the center of each flower a dull yellow eye looks soberly out on the world.

The ground was soft, yielding underfoot, but I left no prints where I walked. So many people have passed here, the woods keep no trace. I found an envelope leaned up against a tree, addressed in an old-fashioned, looping script: "To Stephanie." Inside was a card with a psalm on it: "The Lord is thy keeper. The Lord is thy shade . . ." And, "Congratulations on your confirmation, Always, Adele." The illustration was a watercolor drawing of an improbable sky, all lavender and gilt, with streams of silvery light pouring down from an unlocatable source, some artists's view of nature perfected. I eased it back into its envelope, soft and wet like a large white leaf, folded it once and placed it carefully inside my back pocket.

Bert stopped to wait for me at the fork. One trail, the one to the left, leads out to the highway, and then to town; the other takes the long way down a hill and up again to circle a marshy pond, then finally reenters the dunes further west. I found him standing stark still, studying something before him on the ground. When I caught up with him I saw a small bird, not much bigger than my thumb, lying in the dirt, all black and green, with a patch of raspberry at its throat. One black eye stared upward, fixed on the sky. Its belly squirmed with tiny ants, who went back and forth and in and out with businesslike energy, as if inspecting rental property. Bert took out his sketchbook and began to draw: penciling the line of the beak, fold of wing, and the infinitesimal flurry of the ants; he put these down quickly, for future reference, while the black eye gazed past him into space. He finished drawing it and we went on, taking the right fork, the long way home.

We walked easily side by side as the path widened. Summer has yielded a deep familiarity between us. Now we relax, and take in the world together, at ease in one another, two minds seeing two worlds. Bert notes detail, isolating items of interest, often drawing them in his sketchbook, while I tend to daydream, drifting along between worlds, taking a wide impression of the day.

The pond appeared gradually, magically below us at the foot of the hill. Protected by thick undergrowth and steep banks, its fresh water feeds crayfish and birds, turtles and salamanders, all summer. Mallards are stopping over there now, and black ducks. I've seen a blue-winged teal, and once a great blue heron, shrouded and gaunt, stood for a long while unmoving on shore, like someone thinking over his whole life. Swallows chase after insects in the twilight, and at night the great horned owl feeds on them all, rising up silently in the dark.

The pond is on its way to becoming a freshwater marsh as the grasses and other water plants die and decay along the bottom. I can't tell how fast it is filling in; the water level seems to fluctuate every season. This year it features an abundance of lilies, which like the shallow water, as well as cattails growing along shore. Call it a deep marsh or a shallow pond, either way the ducks don't mind.

The wild things come down to the water: small white butter-flies and red-winged blackbirds, muskrats and weasels and skunks and raccoons, and green and black snails with stripes that curl inward to form a single eye. Another day there might be a wood duck, or even an eagle. In October, the Canada geese will rest here on their migration, making a convention of it, as they paddle the shadows and discuss the progress of their journeys. The pond receives its visitors quietly. All year its population changes. The red squirrels and the chickadees consider themselves residents, but other species come and go; the water holds their wavering reflections. Weeds stand up straight in the still water, grasses tapering to points. Cattails, some slim and firm velvet, others splitting their seams to loose a foam of seeds packed in fluff, stand seven feet tall on woody stems—a stick forest detonating blossom, leaf, seed. An earthworm basks in the path and the sunlight edges away from him. There are territories within territories, overlapping realms of insect, salamander, turtle and fox. All have their claim to this world, ringed by thickets of catbrier and viburnum.

We continued to circle the pond from above, as the path edged along steep banks. Occasional side trails led off into little clearings surrounded by thick scrub. We wandered into one that was littered with beer cans, a plastic bag caught on a bush, and some scattered trash. A circle of scorched stones from a campfire, along with a generally trampled look around the bushes, seemed to indicate repeated, though probably not recent, use. In summer, would-be campers would be driven away by mosquitoes and no-see-ums. Spring and fall bring people into the woods, sometimes drunks from town, or partying high-school kids.

Bert made a sort of harumphing sound, kicking at old ashes in the dirt. "Nice cleanup job, guys," he told the woods sarcastically, as if the villains might still be lurking about to hear. Camping here is strictly against park regulations. Much more of this and there'd be squatter settlements in the woods. Still, I felt oddly pleased by the site. I pictured boys sneaking out of their houses, to light a fire and sit in a circle in the dark, scaring themselves with stories. I pictured young lovers, desperate for the privacy the woods offer. This urge to go off into the woods is old and strong, prehistoric, perhaps even instinctive. I was glad to see the desire prevail against bureaucracy, even a bureaucracy I mostly support.

I plucked the plastic bag from its branch and started putting the beer cans inside it to carry out. "It's probably just kids," I said. "What's the harm? Didn't you ever break any rules?"

"Oh yeah," Bert said. "I forgot you're an outlaw."

The woods end abruptly, sand spilling down the trail between the trees. Scrambling up the bank, we found a sheltered place next to the treetops and sat looking out. Waves of dunes stretched below us, the blue sky touching them all around. Bert took off his shoes and socks, emptied out the sand, and then peeled off his shirt, folded it under his head and lay back. I looked over at him and followed suit. The air was just cool enough to make my skin alert all over: the little hairs on my arms pricked up, and my nipples tightened as a breeze played over my bare chest and Bert ran his fingers lightly across my breasts and belly.

We lay there without talking. Chickadees chipped in the branches and chatted about us; the air grew warmer. Some ducks flew over, black specks on a blue sky. A perfect day, if only it would stay.

Lying there, the stiff grass scratching my back, my elbows puckered from leaning hard on the earth, press of the world against me, and the air moving over my bare breasts and shoulders, I felt inside me a quickening, a longing to reach out and hold the moment. It is all going too fast, I thought. The summer is going, spinning away from us, and where are we? We're like those birds, flown away, a momentary shape of wings passing. The sky vaulted out of reach, blue and bright, and I tried to breathe it in all at once, my head thrown back, everything in me reaching out, opening to take in the fleeting world—an ache I swore I would not feel—September.

I wanted to reach for Bert, make him hold me, ask him what lasts. We live in time, that eats its children. What bond, or plan or promise holds us on this earth, keeps us together? A fly hung overhead, turned to a scarab in the low light, all gold armor glinting in the sun. Bert's breath rose and fell; I could feel his body beside me, alive and strong. I rolled over on top of him, pinning him, rubbing my bare chest against his, catching him by surprise as he lay staring up into the sky. Our mouths opened one on another; his arms tightened around me as I ground my hips into his, breathing harder. We know this at least, the hungers of the body, the power that flows through our flesh and nerves. Kissing, stroking each other deeply, shoulders and neck and waist and ass, we were both lost in a wave of dense, salty desire, our blood rising, swelling us, pushing forward, and he rolled me over and raised himself up on his elbows, his head thrown back. Sliding my shorts down, I opened his jeans and found his cock already hard, pressing forward. It pulsed in my hand like another creature, and I lifted my hips and slid it into me in one motion, moaning.

We fucked under the open sky, rocking and thrusting, in scant shelter beside the woods, given up to want and the need to lose ourselves in our bodies, to be simply alive, sure at least of that. Dumb pleasure, our hip bones rubbing, the sweat shining our chests and arms. Our bodies, these salt houses of memory and desire, know what they want and need; lust rises clear and compelling, finds its way forward without asking for guarantees. Full speed ahead and damn the torpedoes. Maybe this is all we know of giving ourselves over to anything greater. This is what lasts, after all, the endless recurring hunger of life, beating through us. What is, and no more.

We lay back, there under the sky. How is it done—how do you know the bond is true, when do you begin to trust it and let go, to simply live without weighing or asking? Five years? Twenty? You hear of people changing their minds after fifty years ("We were waiting until the children were dead"). People change their minds always, lives break and reform, nothing is set. I entered this marriage as I entered this country, seeking refuge and constancy, wanting ground under my feet. But I chose a home on sand. It's turned out to be a different life than I imagined, a life I move inside of, held, not holding on. But it seems you can't always be thinking of it, wondering, or you won't be living your life. You need to keep two minds, realizing that everything changes, behaving as if it would not.

Bert sat up and took out his sketchbook, turning the page past the bird with the ants marching through its flesh, and began drawing a half-buried tree off to the left. Covered and then exposed by moving dunes, the tips of its branches were honed and whitened by the wind. The marks he makes appear abstract if you don't look too closely, but they are marks of the world. Sitting beside him I could see exactly what he was drawing, the tree top and wisps of grass beside it, drawing them faithfully, realistically, but with a vision so detailed it removes itself from ordinary reality—he will draw just the grain of a log, draw everything swirling and vital in it and you may never see what it is.

I looked away and into the sky. "I lift my eyes unto the hills. From whence cometh my help?" I remembered the beginning of that psalm, the question and answer, but I couldn't summon the rest. I pulled the card from my back pocket. Its garish sky streamed radiance over an implausible, pastel landscape, a different sort of artistic vision. "He shall preserve thy soul," the psalm says. A card for a girl's confirmation. It's a promise, but not what you first think. It's not our lives that are promised. We lose those, going in and out of selves, worlds, seasons, and in losing all, we are protected.

I closed my eyes; of course nothing human lasts. Nothing lasts, but still we are not hurt; our souls cannot be hurt. Can I believe this? I drift. Grassheads lean toward me, bursting with seed. We are meant to come apart in the wind, we are born to lose ourselves. What survives? No promise, no plan, not last year's grass . . . Words of a dead king, pencil marks on a sheaf of paper, these last a little while. "He shall preserve thy soul."

It is still summer by the calendar; neither earlier nor later. It is an act of will to take the changing days as true in their own right, not justified by a progression. It is a moral act to treat the uncertain days of our lives as real and complete. You can see in the moment, the moment passing, or you can see eternity. To be mortal, to love what dies, to let everything you love turn from you and wait for it to turn back. To live in time, safe from harm.

I lay back on the warm earth on a late summer afternoon, safe and mortal, here before time. Now rain patters on the boards over my head, in slow, gentle drops, tapping separately in a light rhythm, gaining speed. I turn into my pillow, at rest here. The folded shirt under my head, warm with my body's heat, the dappled sun and green shade. Weight of his body beside me, our breathing together. The leaves waving up and down on the branches. Sand in the folds of the sheets, the smell of ocean, the smell of rain. The rain falls and the roof catches it and I listen to each impact and diversion, the small reverberations of breaking drops, softly thrumming against the wood. This was my life: It was bright afternoon, and we walked together. We reached the small, quiet pond and circled along shore and could not go down to it, so we went on. We rested on a hilltop. The sun warmed our skin and we turned to one another there in the open and embraced. Our skin was warm and smooth and the little breezes played over us. Sound and motion came back to the place when we finished. The clouds turned round above. Gilded flies hung in the air. I reached up and caught one in my hand and felt its wings against the soft center of my palm, minuscule, intent, beating until I flung it away from me, spinning, the sun catching the filament of its wings as it reeled across the air and disappeared into the wide blue sky, beginning its new life then. The heart rattles, spinning off into the green world.

TWENTY-NINE

Wild Fruits

In late September the shack starts to fill with leaves. Where do they come from, out here where there are no trees? How do they get in? I don't know. They pile up and hang by threads in the corners and crumble into little piles like nests.

They seem very old, stripped down to veins and fragile brown netting. Open the door and they rise and fall in response. Before a storm they rattle warnings, trying to lift and fly away.

The leaves appear some weeks before we leave, and seem to anticipate, or even urge, our going. I push open the door, and there they are. Sweep them down today and there are more tomorrow, though the windows stay shut all night now.

One morning I find a mouse nesting in the corner behind the lime basket. She has chewed up the hem of a green scarf that was folded on the top shelf, and taken small, careful bites from my old wool socks. She waits, gently bold. She only has to stay out of the way, very quietly take what she needs, modestly and without argument, to lie low and wait us out. Sock-fleece and bits of lint and cotton rolled up together make a sleepy warmth, a corner where all is well. Clear it out and she'll begin another. But I let her have it: I'm giving up territory now by inches.

It's the last weekend in September and the air has turned clear and cold. I've come back to spend two nights here before we close up the shack for winter. Ten days ago we moved back to town; our new apartment has three rooms, each of them larger than Euphoria, but crowded with furniture and books they seem small. We're lucky this year: I've found a part-time job that will pay the rent and give me time to write. Pay the rent is about all I will manage, while Bert's somewhat better job will buy groceries, gas, and (incredibly, and I do not scoff) health insurance.

Euphoria has a clean, spare look as the season finishes. Shelves stacked high in May with canned food, soap, matches and batteries are nearly empty now; the woodpile is down to scraps and we're out of coffee. The gaps between the boards are a real presence now, blowing cold air across the floor, leaving little difference between inside and out.

This morning the hill is alive with warblers. They're not shy at all and fly very close to me, looking all around. One with barred wings, a yellow stain along his tail, makes a soft sound ruffling up his wings, then the sweet question in his voice. If I reached out my hand I might touch him. Another one flies past my knee, veering off at the last moment in polite surprise when he notices me. I'm watching wasps crawl over the door frame, exploring cracks under the eaves. They seem obsessed with the spot, mulling it like a question as they crawl in and out, measuring the spaces with their long bodies. They circle each other slowly and seem to drag themselves across the boards.

The wasps arrived as if on some signal, flying dazed and clumsy, drawing stiff circles in the chilly air. Now, as the sun warms them they begin a low drone, coming slowly back to life. These long autumn nights they die over and over, wakening to move painfully. They seem to be looking for a nest this morning, a place to settle in for winter, though winter will surely kill most of them.

These are the golden days, the last ones. One last thing after another happens, and every morning it seems somebody turns up missing. The rosehips are deep orange, and there are small white flowers along the ground under the grass. The seaside goldenrod is brilliant; the dune grass pales, green and blond strands mixed together, the heavy, seeded heads leaning into the hills.

Gulls congregate on the high dune, little black dots against the sand, arrayed as if awaiting orders. They aren't going anywhere. But whales are swimming down the Gulf Stream toward winter feeding grounds. Monarch butterflies have headed to Mexico, and swarms of dragonflies flee west with swift intent.

When did the song sparrow leave? We heard him all summer; a soloist as big as a salt shaker, he clung to the top of the bayberry proclaiming his dominion all day long. Then one day he stopped, and flew around feeding peacefully on seeds, tearing the roses apart with great good cheer. A quiet fellow, unassuming. I didn't even see him go.

The terns gave up their hard-fought territory on the beach just as casually. All summer they defended their ground with religious zeal, driving off intruders with shrill cries and sharply aimed dives. Then one day it was over. They plodded along the beach, sedate and mild, indifferent to everyone. They stayed around a while, fishing and diving, and gradually drifted away to join up with larger flocks just in from the north. They waited for the next signal that would tell them when to go, and when it came they were off for South America without a backward look.

They're gone now, and the red-winged blackbirds too, who were so noisy and so noticeable all summer, and that flock of tree swallows rising and falling in nervous waves down in the valley must be on its way out of town. I have never seen so many together. Winter finches pass through, and warblers, hundreds of thousands of them, headed south in mixed flocks.

Next week we will pack up the last of our gear and nail up shutters over the windows. Sealed tight, dark inside, Euphoria rides out the winter storms, rocking, while the sand blows all around. When we're gone, the place returns to itself, to a greater wildness.

Our time here is bounded by the seasons. The whole Outer

Cape, particularly these dunes, has a long history of settlement, but this land has never been permanently occupied. Fishermen, beachcombers, hunters and gatherers, Coast Guardsmen, artists, tourists and loners have come here, gone away, and returned. I wonder what the meaning of home is for any of us migrants. All populations here, human and otherwise, change with the seasons. There is a strength to this place that cannot be owned, but only inhabited—as animals inhabit each place in its own time, in full confidence of belonging.

The summer tenants had barely packed up their last picnics and taken half-damp towels down from the line when we moved into our winter quarters. We found a child's swimsuit and a half bottle of dark rum left behind. The town is quiet now, but not quite shut down for winter; it's a peaceful time, good for walking the harbor and empty beaches; there's plenty of space between one person and another for once. I return to town in circular fashion, my range identified within sight of the water tower and the Pilgrim Monument. I live in one improvised home after another, becoming resident without ever holding a deed, or even a year-round lease.

Mornings, it's cold enough to light a fire. All summer we saved up paper: newspapers and letters, and a sad-looking box of discarded notebook pages written over and crossed out—a testament to my struggles here. I begin my fire with paper, burning words to drive off the chill and ignite deeper memories in wood. Black and white of old records, tide charts, ads, births, deaths, and deliberations of the zoning board: these burn so easily, crumble and smoke and send fire into the sticks and wood scraps I use for kindling. All the strange pieces we picked up along shore end up in the woodpile, along with stakes from the old snow fence we thought would hold back a moving dune one winter. The weight of sand burst its wires and left the pickets standing like broken teeth. The wood catches fire, detonating orange and red blossoms that crack and open and give off light. Old shingles, scraps of driftwood, boards thrown off boats, all these Euphoria burns in its stove, using the stored heat of the sun. Closed up, behind the metal door, the fire gulps and gasps, drinking air, making light out of the past.

The marsh hawk is back. I see her flying past the window and go to the door to look out. Her wings beat shallow and slow as she tacks back and forth over the tall grasses. I remember: there has always been a marsh hawk at Euphoria. Winters, she nests in the woods near town; we'll be neighbors again then. She flies over the valley, aware of me now, uninterested. She listens instead for mice and voles, what runs along the ground. The grass grows quiet under her spell. Alive, every heartbeat a sign, a danger just to breathe. Something will come to her.

I look up: there is an invisible wire between us, pulled straight from my breast, hooked into her flight. She tests it, wheeling, circling back. The line goes slack and drops as she dips in front of the hill; it's pulled up tight again as she rises, pulling my breath up into my throat. Her wings beat harder now, and she lifts upward, pulling, straining, until the wire snaps and flies up into the sky.

Then there is nothing holding me. I stand in the open door, the sun on my face, looking up into all that blue.

UNIVERSITY PRESS OF NEW ENGLAND

publishes books under its own imprint and is the publisher for Brandeis University
Press, Dartmouth College, Middlebury College Press, University of New Hampshire,
Tufts University, and Wesleyan University Press.

Library of Congress Cataloging-in-Publication Data

Huntington, Cynthia, 1951–

  The salt house : a summer on the dunes of Cape Cod / Cynthia
Huntington.

      p.   cm.

    ISBN 0–87451–934–9 (alk. paper)

    1. Huntington, Cynthia, 1951–   —Homes and haunts—Massachusetts—
Cape Cod. 2. Women poets, American, 20th century Biography.
3. Cape Cod (Mass.)—Social life and customs.   4. Natural history—
Massachusetts—Cape Cod.   5. Sand dunes—Massachusetts—Cape Cod.
6. Cottages—Massachusetts—Cape Cod.   7. Summer—Massachusetts—
Cape Cod.   I. Title.

PS3558.U517Z49   1999

811'.54 dc21   99-20680

[B]